FLY FISHING THE SURF

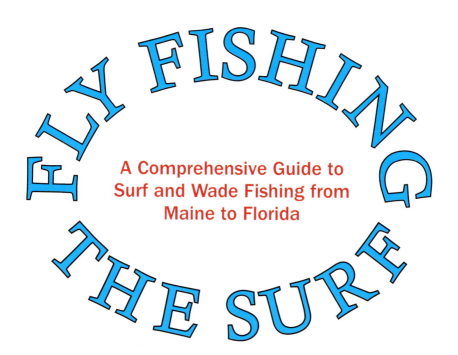

FLY FISHING THE SURF

A Comprehensive Guide to
Surf and Wade Fishing from
Maine to Florida

ANGELO PELUSO

Skyhorse Publishing

Copyright © 2013 by Angelo Peluso
All photos are copyrighted to Angelo Peluso unless otherwise noted.

All Rights Reserved. No part of this book may be reproduced in any manner without the express written consent of the publisher, except in the case of brief excerpts in critical reviews or articles. All inquiries should be addressed to Skyhorse Publishing, 307 West 36th Street, 11th Floor, New York, NY 10018.

Skyhorse Publishing books may be purchased in bulk at special discounts for sales promotion, corporate gifts, fund-raising, or educational purposes. Special editions can also be created to specifications.

For details, contact the Special Sales Department, Skyhorse Publishing, 307 West 36th Street, 11th Floor, New York, NY 10018
or
info@skyhorsepublishing.com.

Skyhorse® and Skyhorse Publishing® are registered trademarks of s GSkyhorse Publishing, Inc.®, a Delaware corporation.

www.skyhorsepublishing.com

10 9 8 7 6 5 4 3 2 1

Library of Congress Cataloging-in-Publication Data is available on file.

ISBN: 978-1-62087-596-4

Printed in China

This book is dedicated to all who share a passion for fly fishing, and to all who are intrigued by the edge of the surf line and the glorious gamefish that swim in salt water. And to my Labrador retriever, Bailey, who was at my side every step of the way throughout this entire project.

Contents

Preface

At Water's Edge

Some may refer to the condition as an obsession, but there is no doubt that I am addicted to salt water. Aside from the love of family, close friends, and my Labrador retriever, nothing quite touches my soul or invigorates my spirit like being physically part of a coastal ecosystem. Were I forced to chose only one water-based activity to pursue for my remaining days on this earth, it would be wading in salt water with a fly rod in hand, casting to some magnificent gamefish. It matters not the species nor where I fish but rather the scene and how the complete experience unfolds. Fly fishing is truly a sport that is all about the journey of discovery and not simply the destination where one arrives. There is something magical and captivating about being in the water with a direct connection between the end of your fly line and a creature of the sea. To set the hook and feel the vibrations of throbbing life move straight from the water to your hands is as good as it gets. The connection is holistically aquatic when the angler is standing in the same environment as the fish. After making the acquaintance of your opponent, you get to hold it, one hand gently beneath its belly, the other firmly grasping a thick tail. For a moment in time, angler and fish are one, until a quick sweep of a powerful tail propels it back home. From that moment on the connection cannot be broken. In my mind this is the pinnacle of sport fishing.

When I was a kid growing up in New York City, I would often venture to City Island or Orchard Beach on the outer reaches of the Bronx to cast a baited hook as far as I could with the expectation of enticing any fish willing to eat my modest offering. Usually it was a piece of sandworm or bloodworm or a hunk of clam. If my grandmother had any leftover bits of fresh squid, shrimp, or scallops that weren't transformed into some Neapolitan culinary masterpiece, I'd stick them on the hook, too. While I waited for flounder, tomcod, striped bass, or bluefish to bite, I would often contemplate the possibility that someday I might own a boat and be able to fish well beyond my longest cast, in places where I knew the trophies had to be. Surely, fish were out there in distant secret hideaways, not in here where I stood wishfully waiting for some straggler to intercept a deceptively free meal.

Eventually the day came when I was able to afford my own boat. Rigged and ready for action, I pointed the bow toward the mouth of Port Jefferson Harbor off the Long Island Sound, mashed the throttle forward, and broke free of the shackles that had bound me to shore. Freedom from being landlocked was the gift this hull and engine would bestow upon me, an emancipation that would translate into more and bigger fish. I glanced back well behind the boat's wake and waved goodbye to the shoreline, a big smile stretched across my face. My sights that day were set on a fabled offshore haunt in the center of the Long Island Sound, aptly called the Middle Grounds. I had heard all the stories of supersize striped bass and gargantuan bluefish that roamed the "grounds" and the nearby shoal, all too willing to eat one's bait. Cow bass and gator blues would soon relent to my liberation from the land. Upon reaching this storied fishing hole I set anchor and began to cast, and cast . . . and cast. After several hours of fishing, not a single fish was tempted by my artificial offerings. Reluctantly, I pulled up anchor and slowly worked my way back toward port feeling defeated. Disappointment would mark my first offshore adventure.

But a funny thing happened on the way in from the legendary fishing grounds that had just served up a major-league skunk. As the shoreline came into view, I noticed a long line of boats fishing directly off one of the beaches I often fished. I pushed forward on the throttle and steered in the direction of the growing fleet. Much to my amazement most rods on all the boats were doubled over, and those anglers who had not yet hooked up were casting. They were in their boats and casting toward the beach; a beach from which I had just escaped. Striped bass, bluefish, and weakfish were blitzing along the entire stretch of water precisely where it met the land and the sand. Despite my desire to seek new fishing haunts way out yonder, the temptation of fish literally at my feet was too great. I quickly joined in on the action Talk about the ultimate irony. With my dreamboat now underfoot—my platform to the deep blue sea—here I was casting toward a beach I had longed to flee. But catching a variety of prized gamefish at a rapid rate had me swallow my pride. The next few days found me back in the same location, at times fishing but a cast away from the sand, and waving to beachcombers as they strolled by. I remember thinking: I could have waded out this far. That great shoreline bite continued for about a week, until fish moved off the beach and into deeper water. I was glad then that I had a boat so I could follow those fish around, but the memories of that in-close fishing lingered and to a great extend were catalysts that molded the future direction of my angling habits and preferences.

I have enjoyed some absolutely spectacular fly fishing from boats throughout the course of my angling career but, not surprisingly, I always find myself gravitating back toward the surf, flats, and shallow backwaters. I've grown to understand that I would much rather be in water than on it when fishing. A well-worn pair of favorite waders and wading boots patched with numerous silicone and duct tape repairs are testimony of that proclivity. That gear is a permanent fixture in the back of my truck.

I spend most of the early season in the Northeast, wading, kayaking to surf and backwater locations, or exploring flats where I can simply walk into the water and cast to my heart's content. When I visit other areas along more southerly stretches of the East Coast, similar scenarios play out. I still very much enjoy standing on the bow of a shallow-draft boat sight casting to cruising and feeding fish, but more often than not you will find me somewhere in the water. I am drawn there naturally and I believe it is part of my core genetic make-up. Perhaps my DNA helix contains a few throwback genes to a primal time and place when ancestors searched shallow water for sustenance. Although my contemporary motivation is recreational angling—not survival—that distant bond is renewed each time I step from the edge of land and enter the sea. The merging is always seamless and harmonious, and in naturally perfect transition. It's as if that is where I was meant to be. With fly rod in hand, the magic that ensues knows no boundaries. It is a one-act play that keeps repeating over and over, never losing the impact of its similar but very different endings. Whether it is the Long Island surf, the mouth of an Alaskan coastal river, the flats of the Yucatan Peninsula, the beaches of Florida's Sanibel and Captiva Islands, or any tidal waters in between, each fish caught in this manner makes the experience genuinely unique.

But it is more than just about the fish. I feel rejuvenated around water—especially when wading in the liquid medium with a 9-foot 9-weight at the ready. My inner spirit responds instantly when summoned to the surf, the shoreline of a quiet back bay, or the enchanting allure of a tidal flat. I am very much enticed by the call of resident and migrating gamefish, and equally so by the timeless, seductive sounds of the surf's graceful rhythms. Enveloped by salt water, I am connected to the influences of eternal and perpetual tides, a flow that has proven to be an extraordinary elixir. Through countless flyfishing exploits, I have grown in harmony with daily and seasonal tidal movements. My movements flow in concert with the height of a proxigean spring tide, the low water of a quarter-moon neap tide, and all the daily tides that endlessly flood and ebb. To follow fish from the edge of the surf line or from any wadable water has become my primary flyfishing quest. It is what I prefer to do over all other forms of angling. That pursuit has enabled me to develop a bond with the varied species of fish that frequent inshore waters. In the Northeast, I eagerly await their annual arrival in the spring and lament their departure in late fall. If I've not been satiated with the fishing and catching at that point, I often choose to follow the fish on their migratory journey south.

To an extent, the fish and I engage in similar passage. They travel well-worn routes in perpetual processions seeking food, natal breeding grounds, or more suitable habitats within which to thrive. I too am driven to those same waters to cast a fly and to receive much needed nourishment that can't be achieved by simply drinking eight glasses of water daily. Each time I step from the edge and become one with the hydrogen oxygen compound, I am recharged and all in the world is good once again.

—Angelo Peluso, at the Long Island Sound, winter 2013

Introduction

O ne of the most spectacular mass migrations in the entire natural world occurs off an iconic north Atlantic promontory known as Montauk Point.
The event takes place in the fall of each year and is described by many who
witness it as larger-than-life. Untold numbers of gamefish, baitfish, birds, and anglers
all converge upon this piece of priceless real estate to partake in an annual ritual. For
those fortunate enough to fish amidst this exhilarating grandeur, or to simply bear
witness to the event, there are no words to adequately describe what takes place. I
have often been there, a bit player in the scene, when the fly fishing is so good no
superlatives do it justice. Many of the uninitiated may sneer at one's recounting of a
phenomenal fall day of fishing off The Point and charge the stories as being nothing
more than fishermen's hyperbole. But Montauk is a place where fantasy meets reality.

Surf fishing is a rewarding pastime for anglers of all levels. (Photo credit: Rich Santos)

At times it can be like the Disney World of fly fishing, an angling amusement park where dreams magically come true.

As unbelievable as the fishing is from a boat, it can be equally as astounding from the beach. Montauk is known in many circles as the Surf-Fishing Capital of the World, and it lives up to that reputation. The majority of surf anglers typically employ traditional gear: long surf sticks matched to spinning or conventional casting reels. But for each year over the past fifteen or twenty fall seasons, increasing numbers of fly rodders have lined up along the sand beaches adjacent to The Point, or have taken up positions on the rocks and boulders that are hallmarks of the area. The primary quarry are striped bass, false albacore, and bluefish that appear like clockwork and in mesmerizing numbers. Whether standing on the deck of a boat or perched upon an oversized glacial rock, you can often hear the fish coming well before you see them. It is usually the sound of fleeing, jumping, and skittering baitfish under attack—literally tens of thousands, perhaps millions, that reach one's ears first. But even that advance warning is sometimes not enough to prepare you for the spectacle that shortly follows. The first time I saw it, I couldn't believe my eyes: an acre or more of striped bass, mouths agape on the water's surface, fins and tails exposed, tearing through balled-up and hapless bay anchovies. I was so captivated by the moment that my fishing buddy, who instantly hooked up with a bass, asked if I was planning to watch or cast. I chose to watch for a while, reveling in the majestic moment, and then I made a cast. It was almost as guaranteed a hook-up as one could ever expect in fishing. Similar sights and experiences unfolded that day with false albacore, bluefish, and combinations of all three species, a veritable hat trick of fly rod-friendly gamefish.

Although the Montauk surf is unique in its class, it does not stand alone as a first-class fly-fishing destination. The entire length of the East Coast of the United States plays host to inshore fisheries that welcome the fly angler. From the tip of the rugged Maine shoreline to the fine sand beaches of south Florida and the Gulf Coast, opportunities abound for those choosing to target gamefish with a fly. Some locations are equally renowned as Montauk, but many are lesser gems just waiting to be mined. Each of the eastern coastal states, north to south, has its signature beaches that call to the surf fly angler to come visit. These are places such as: Maine's Old Orchard Beach; New Hampshire's Hampton Beach; the beaches of Cape Cod, Massachusetts; Rhode Island's Block Island; Connecticut's Penfield Reef; Long Island's Fire Island National Seashore; New York City's Jamaica Bay; Island Beach State Park in New Jersey; Delaware's Fenwick Island State Park, Assateague Island in Maryland; Virginia's Chincoteague Island, VA; North Carolina's Outer Banks; South Carolina coastal lowlands; Georgia's Tybee Island; and the pristine flats of the Florida Keys. These are locations where local and visiting anglers can find exceptional wade fishing with the fly rod.

During my tenure as an avid fly fisherman and member of the outdoors media, I have had opportunities to talk with many other anglers up and down the East Coast. While the Southeast and Gulf Coast states have long and storied histories of saltwater fly fishing, the height of the sport's popularity in the Northeast occurred with the recovery of striped bass stocks in the early 1990s. Solid year classes of fine fly rod-size fish were in abundance. Bass, bluefish, weakfish, false albacore, and Atlantic bonito made up the core of gamefish species that helped recruit new entrants into saltwater fly fishing and convert many freshwater fly anglers. All the while participation continued to grow in the traditional markets of the Southeast and Gulf Coast.

The sport enjoyed a period of rapid and sustained growth. The only factor that contributed to a halt in that expansion was the Great Recession that gained momentum in 2008. Much of the recreational fishing and boating industries dropped back down into first gear or reverse, with the goal of capital preservation and surviving the economic crisis, and recreational anglers did somewhat the same. There was one notable exception, however. Despite all the down-trending red arrows, there was a slightly upward blip on the screen of one industry segment: surf and wade fishing in all its forms. The reasons were obvious. Many boat anglers were downsizing, selling, or going to smaller motorized craft and kayaks to achieve a more favorable economic return on their fishing time. Boat financing was virtually nonexistent, so credit was not available for boat purchases. Gas prices caused many anglers to cut back on longer trips, and employers were demanding extra time of their employees, to do more with less. The net effect of all this was that anglers were forced to make alternative fishing decisions. Many entered the world of surf fishing due to the relative ease of entry into the sport, while many of those who were already in the sport went looking for ways to supplement their fishing tools and tactics. Fly fishing the surf was the answer to those needs. The relatively low cost of entry into the sport and the ability to simply wade into the playing field were two of the most significant reasons for that phenomenon. Other contributing factors included technology and the impact it had on reducing the cost of fly rods and reels. It was no longer necessary to take a second mortgage on one's home to buy high-quality fly rods and reels. And while there are still very high-end rods and reels on the market, many manufacturers have revamped their product lines and come out with affordable gear targeted at new entrants into the sport.

When I took my first flyfishing trip to the shores of wild Alaskan rivers in the late 1980s, it was not unreasonable to spend $500 or more on suitable travel rods. Today it is possible to buy better rods for half that amount, and there are many manufacturers within the marketplace to choose from. The same is true of fly reels and lines. Additionally, and equally as important, much of the mystique has been removed from a sport that once perpetuated a belief that you had to be one part shaman and one part magician to cast a fly. Once anglers move beyond the purity of dry-fly fishing with gossamer leaders, they can discover the amazing world of fly fishing in salt water. And today, there are many more resources available to the aspiring fly angler than there were back when I entered the sport: clubs; instructional videos; descriptive books; Internet websites; even casting coaches. The fact of the matter is that if you are coordinated enough to hit a beach ball with a Louisville Slugger, you can easily learn to fly cast. From there all it takes is practice, a modicum of discipline, and a willingness to learn.

Many saltwater boat and surf anglers are often reluctant to get involved in fly fishing for fear of failure. That is pure nonsense. The most important attribute of a good surf fly angler is to first be a good general angler. What that means is having an ability to read water; understand tides, currents, and weather; have in-depth knowledge of baitfish and gamefish, their movements, and their behaviors; and spend time on the water practicing the craft. Fly fishing's primary purpose is to stimulate fish to strike a fraudulent bait made from feathers, fur, synthetics, and various combinations of those materials. Under the best of circumstances that is not always an easy task. The best fly anglers have learned to manipulate their flies to replicate a life-form and create the illusion that their offering is the real deal. While the process and tackle may be different, that objective is not unlike the process used by spinning and conventional fisherman casting plugs, tins, and an endless variation of plastic baits. Unfortunately, some neophytes—and even more experienced fly anglers—often get frustrated with fly fishing from the surf and revert back to other forms of tackle, limiting their use of fly gear to just bluebird and easy fishing days. That is a mistake. We learn as much, if not more, from the challenging days as we do from the great ones.

It is my hope that this book will open up the entire world of fly fishing the surf and the enormous promise this form of angling can offer. One need only look at the coastal landscape from Maine to Florida to appreciate the full potential of the sport. If that isn't enough motivation, then simple exploration of the waters of the Northeast, the mid-Atlantic states, and the Southeast will lead an angler to a goldmine of remarkable gamefish species. The list is impressive, and can literally keep a surf fly angler busy for an entire lifetime or two.

What type of fish are we talking about? In the Northeast, the beach fishing headliners are striped bass, bluefish, weakfish, false albacore, bonito, and fluke. The Southeast, meanwhile, offers up snook, redfish, spotted seatrout, bonefish, permit, and even tarpon to the wading angler; while in the center of the East Coast, the mid-Atlantic states proffer not only their indigenous species of gamefish but become a tantalizing convergence point for northern species moving south and southern species traveling north. Match to that the incredible diversity of baitfish that flies can readily replicate and the formula for success is proven.

Productive surf- and wade-fishing locations can be found in your own backyard if you know what to look for.

In the song, "Coastal Confessions," Jimmy Buffett sings about being a tidal pool explorer from the days of his misspent youth. I guess you can say I am a tidal pool explorer too, looking for the next puddle of water that might hold fish or some existential truth about why some of us were put on this planet to cast flies. Given that all water has its appeal and unique attraction, this book defines surf in its broadest sense to include not only traditional ocean-facing open beaches but any water into which a fly angler can wade. That spectrum of water includes: flats, marshes, backcountry, harbors, bays, sound beaches, tidal creeks, river mouths, and any other places where one's wading boots can find access. I've caught fish on flies in the best of places—idyllic and aesthetic settings—and in some of the least likely places one would expect to find any self-respecting gamefish. Regardless of location, all it takes is me stepping in the water, casting a fly, and hooking a fish to make any spot a magical one.

The vision for this book was born not just from that acknowledgment but from the fact that fly fishing from the surf is a rewarding and at times highly effective form of angling. I do enjoy fishing from my boat and I do enjoy paddling my kayak, but I love fishing from the edge of the surf. And I find irresistible the connection the sport makes with our primitive ancestors who fished for subsistence. Long before there were boats, those ancient fishermen walked into the unknown to catch their next meal. Many did so with bone hooks adorned with fur or feathers—primordial flies. The use of an artificial fly technically extends back that far to those ancients who first crossed the great Bering Land Bridge from Asia to what is now Alaska. But the roots of more contemporary flies have an ancestry that traces back to early Macedonia. Those anglers too cast flies upon waters they waded. While those early anglers were driven by survival instincts, and we today by the sport and challenge of it all, those primitive roots still connect us to a great sport. So please join me now as we explore the world of fly fishing the surf.

Chapter One

Tackling the Surf

Selecting a Fly Rod

Whenever I suggest to my wife that she has one too many pairs of shoes, she gives me her patented laser stare and counter-suggests that we take a look inside my tackle closets and count fly rods. I will admit that I have a sizable collection of fly rods, and I remind my spouse that while she has only two feet, I need to be prepared to catch diverse species of fish under many different circumstances. My response is always met with a total lack of empathy. I have been fly fishing for most of my life, and it is only natural that I have acquired a variety of tackle over the years. After all, fly fishermen, like duck hunters, tend to be pack rats, and I do have a sweet spot for fly rods; there is a natural inclination to hoard them. Yet despite the variety and number of rods that I own, it is easy to distinguish the favorites and the ones that get called into action most frequently.

Those rods either sit in the rod rack, at the ready with reels attached and line strung, or rest at the front of the closet within easy reach. There are three favorite trout rods that have seen more than their fair share of brookies, browns, and rainbows; there's a freshwater bass-bugging rod that has become a great old friend; there are my trusty three- and four-piece Alaska and travel rods that have shared some exciting adventures; and lastly, my saltwater outfits for local waters. The last of those rod categories represents the most sizable part of my collection, and with good reason: much of my fly fishing is done in salt water, most often from the surf. That collection of rods includes two-, three-, and four-piece sticks.

Given the assortment of rods in the marketplace, making a selection, especially for a first rod, can seem like a daunting task. I am often asked by aspiring saltwater anglers what one all-round fly rod would be the best choice for their surf-fishing needs. My response is always the same: a 9-foot 9-weight with a moderate or fast action. That selection is ideal if you can only have one rod for fly fishing the surf. A

9-foot 9-weight (9/9) is a versatile and effective fishing tool. Over the course of my surf fishing, I have caught a wide array of gamefish on that rod type: striped bass, bluefish, Atlantic bonito, false albacore, summer flounder, redfish, snook, bonefish, jacks, and a host of others. Further validation of that choice is that within the salt-water flyfishing community the nines are a resounding favorite among those anglers who fish the surf.

The 9/9 is comparable to a utility infielder, in that the rod can be used effective-ly for a variety of gamefish and can handle many circumstances that you'll encounter when fishing the surf. While that category of rod is my go-to tool, I will often choose other rods for specialty applications or simply to increase my fishing enjoyment. The scope of my saltwater surf fly-rod arsenal spans a range from 7-weight rods to beefy 12-weights, the core being the 8-, 9-, and 10-weights. There are times when I will select a 7-weight for seatrout, small bluefish, and shad; while an 8-weight can be a fun tool for early season striped bass in back bays or flats, when smaller baits and matching flies are the ticket. I will sometimes opt for a 10-weight to play catch and release with stout and powerful little tunny; an 11-weight can help overcome the wind-in-the face syndrome that often accompanies fishing the open surf; and a 12-weight is ideal for those times when I might encounter large gamefish such as tarpon in the surf. Yet, more often than not a fast-action 9-weight will be what I cast. Bear in mind there is no need to run out and buy one of each until you progress to a level where there is a specialty need. For all practical purposes, a 9- or 10-weight rod will suffice for most of your surf-fishing needs.

A fly rod is a very effective surf fishing tool.

Fundamentals of Fly-Rod Selection

It is usually the fly rod that grabs the attention of newcomers to saltwater surf fishing. Typically, the rod is selected first, then a decision is made on a matching reel. While both need to be purchased with the other in mind, the rod tends to get top billing.

A fly rod's primary purpose is to cast a fly line to which a leader and fly are attached. Unlike spinning or conventional bait-casting gear, where the weight of the lure or terminal tackle pulls line from the reel to make a cast, a fly rod is engineered to propel the weight of the fly line. Both rod and line are calibrated so that they are matched to maximize loading of the rod and the power-casting stroke. In the hands of a skilled and practiced caster, distance and precise fly placement can be consistently achieved.

An equally significant function of a fly rod is to manage the fly line. Maintaining constant contact with the line, whether in flight or on the water, is critical. Lose touch with the line during the cast or the retrieve and you will lose opportunities to properly present a fly or to hook a fish. One example of crucial line control is when a fly is drifted in strong current, such as is often encountered around a jetty point or a sand bar. In those situations, it is imperative to keep the fly drifting in a natural manner with the flow of the current. The rod is used to mend line or reposition line back up current so that the fly assumes a natural posture and drifts unimpeded with the flow of water. Using the rod to mend line prevents a fly from rising unnaturally in the water column. This and other line control techniques will be discussed in greater detail later in the book.

Rod, reel, and line all work in concert to cast and fight fish.   (Photo credit: Laura Pisano)

Another of a fly rod's principal duties is to strike and hook fish. In saltwater surf fishing, this typically occurs through the process of strip-setting, where the rod is lifted while simultaneously pulling back on the line to set the hook. Once the hook is secure, the rod then transforms into a tool to fight and land the fish. Contrary to the beliefs of some, a fly rod is a powerful fishing implement, and it can subdue substantial quarry when in the hands of an experienced angler. Many who are new to the sport are usually amazed at how much pressure can be applied to big fish hooked on a fly rod. Albeit from boats, big tarpon, tuna, marlin, sharks, and many other offshore species are regularly landed on fly rods. For the average surf angler, a fly rod is more than capable of fighting and landing inshore gamefish.

While most anglers have a preference for single-handed fly rods, some who fish the surf prefer a two-handed Spey rod or a switch rod, a hybrid between a Spey and single-handed stick. The inherent advantages of these rods are longer casts, a degree of enhanced line control, and enhanced fish-fighting benefits. The two-handed grips also allow for increased leverage with the back and forward casts.

The Flexibility Factor

One potentially perplexing aspect of fly-rod selection is that of action. It needn't be. In its simplest terms, fly-rod action equates to the flexibility of the rod blank and how much it bends when under stress. That stress is a function of the casting process, specifically the back cast. A fly rod needs to load or store energy that is released upon the forward-casting stroke. That energy load provides the power to let the line travel its full course. The actions of contemporary, high-tech fly rods are measured in degrees of "flex," or how the rods bend during the back cast. While one prominent rod manufacturer has developed a flex index for ease of comparing the action of its line of fly rods, there is no uniform industry index to compare flex between rod manufacturers. The true test comes with one's own understanding of the dynamics of flex and comparison casting to feel the differences in actions. Fly-rod action is categorized in one of three designations: full-flex, or slow action; mid-flex, or moderate action; and tip-flex, or fast action.

FULL-FLEX

Most of my freshwater trout rods are full-flex, having deep and sustained bends throughout much of the rod blank, butt to tip. That characteristic is beneficial for in-close fishing and for subtle presentations, a requisite in crystal-clear spring creeks. A full-flex rod is also forgiving to varied casting styles and offers gentle hook setting with delicate tippets. This style action is designed into classic bamboo trout rods and most small stream graphite rods. For all practical purposes, full-flex rods are not a preferred choice for the saltwater surf angler.

MID-FLEX

This action is somewhat of a compromise and provides for a versatile flex, one that begins about midway through the rod. It offers a blend of butt section strength that is beneficial when fighting big fish, and a moderate overall bend that contributes to easier casting. This type action performs well in most surf-fishing situations and is friendly to a range of casting strokes. It is an ideal action for the angler who may be limited to one rod for the surf, since it can respond effectively to varied fishing conditions. A rod with this action can easily transform from one that fishes big flies aggressively to another that tosses crustacean patterns to wary and cruising fish on the flats.

TIP-FLEX

Fast-action fly rods have grown tremendously in popularity and are often the first choice among saltwater anglers. One of the principal reasons is that "fast" rods have all the action contained in the tip section. This action is much stiffer than either full-flex or mid-flex rods but has the capability to generate optimal line speed. That trait is often beneficial when quick, long casts are required, or when line speed is needed to overcome wind. Tip-flex rods are considered the most powerful of the three categories of actions and, while they can generate substantial power during the cast, they can, nonetheless, be a bit troublesome for newcomers to get used to. This action is a lot less forgiving than either of the two slower flexes. With practice and familiarity, tip-flex rods are ideal choices.

What Piece Rod?

Another consideration when acquiring a fly rod for surf fishing is sectional construction and the number of pieces to the rod. Science of design and new-age materials have allowed for multipiece rods to perform as flawlessly as one-piece rods. Custom one-piece fly rods can still be built to angler specifications but, to be candid, there is really no need for that unless you are fixated on not having any ferrules. Again, you need to consider whether you want an all-round, one-size-fits-all rod or a specialty rod. For fly fishing the surf, two-, three-, and even four-piece rods will fit the bill well. My personal preference is for two pieces, but three- and four-section rods are equally effective. The fact is that with today's engineering—and that includes superb ferrule connections—multipiece rods perform as well as one-piece rods. An added benefit of multipiece rods is that they're easy to travel with. With the quality of rods currently in the marketplace, and the number of top-tier manufacturers producing high-performance products, surf fly anglers should have no concerns about multisection rods.

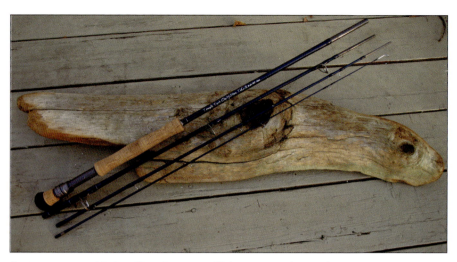

Contemporary multi-piece fly rods are as efficient as one-piece rods.

A Matter of Materials

Fly rods are primarily constructed of bamboo, fiberglass, graphite, boron, or composite materials. Like many of my generation, my first fishing rod was a bamboo cane pole. Rigged with a length of line, bobber, hook, and minnow or worm, it was an effective tool for panfish and small bass. I would even use it in salt water for snapper bluefish. But would I use a custom bamboo fly rod today for saltwater surf fishing? No! Some anglers do as a novelty, but in general classic bamboo rods have no place on the saltwater surf-fishing scene. While there is a robust bamboo market for custom freshwater rods, the harsh saltwater environment can be disastrous for that rod-building material.

Fiberglass broke onto the rod-building scene as the material of choice after World War Two. The Shakespeare Company was the first to commercially offer fly rods made from fiberglass with their "Wonder Rods." And wonders they were at the time, being strong, durable, light, and inexpensive when compared to custom bamboo rods. A testament to their durability is that I still have my first bass-bugging Wonder Rod and it performs as well today as it did many years ago. Fiberglass is still used in rod building. Despite the introduction of more advanced materials, there is still a handful of traditional surf anglers that prefers fiberglass over other materials. Many of these anglers claim that the softness of the rod flex enhances the action of plugs. Within the flyfishing community there are also those who have a soft spot for glass rods. If you happen to be one of them, some good fiberglass fly rods are still around that can be put into service for surf fishing. Fiberglass is also used as a supporting material in graphite rods, adding strength to an already durable material.

Graphite is far and away the most popular rod-building material in use today and is ideal for saltwater fly fishing. Over the years it has evolved to the point where the current generation of graphite rods features some of the strongest and lightest ever made. Without getting too far into the science and engineering of graphite, fly rods made from that material have progressed from epoxy-based resins to thermoplastic resins, and most recently to nano-resins. Simply, those advancements translate into stronger rods, constructed of less material, generating lighter weight.

Some manufacturers offer composite blends of boron and graphite. Boron fibers are light, stiff, and compress less under the stress of casting. Those characteristics result in increased strength and power. Most applications of boron are to the butt sections of rods, adding to the fish-fighting capability of those fly rods and the ability to more easily lift line off the water during the initial stage of the back cast.

In the final analysis, the number of rod sections to choose from comes down to personal preference. If you are in the market for your first surf fly rod, either a 9- or 10-weight graphite rod, or graphite/boron blend, with a mid- or tip-flex should be high on the list. The choice of two-, three-, or four-piece rods is more a function of portability than performance, so that comes down to individual choice. When deciding on your purchase, make certain to test cast the rod before buying. Under ideal buying conditions you should cast the rod with a reel similar to the one you will use, so you can gauge balance, with a matched fly line. A simulated fly should also be attached to offer a degree of resistance that better approximates real casting conditions.

Selecting a Fly Reel

In what seems like the very distant past when freshwater trout dominated the flyfishing scene, a fly reel was considered nothing more than a line storage device. Smaller trout and even bass weren't viewed as much of a threat to the simple pawl and click drag mechanisms. But as fly fishing expanded and large steelhead and rainbows, Atlantic and Pacific salmon, pike, muskies, and exotic freshwater gamefish were targeted, reels took on a different purpose. That change was further stimulated by saltwater fly fishing, where bigger, stronger, and more diverse species were pursued.

Big fish required that the fly reel transform into a vital flyfishing tool that not only stored line but aided in the process of fighting fish. Stronger and more durable drag systems were designed, some totally hermetically sealed to prevent corrosion damage from unforgiving salt water. Fly reels have since become as scrutinized as fly rods during the purchase process. Reels are sized to the lines they accommodate, allowing for not only the line to be spooled but also for adequate backing. Depending on species fished and amount of backing required, reels can typically adapt to one line size up. For example, a reel designated for a 9-weight line and 250 yards of backing might also handle a 10-weight line with less backing. Furthermore, different type lines have varying diameters, and depending on the line selected, more or less line might fill the spool. But for general use, one should stay within the parameters defined by the manufacturer specifications.

When selecting a fly reel for the surf, one of the key design features is that of increased line capacity and rate of line retrieval. Large arbor spools are preferable for achieving these objectives. Arbor size is expressed as a measurement from reel plate to reel plate, while deep diameter spools have a greater depth of spool. Both spool configurations offer increased line capacity for fly line and backing. One the most significant advantages of a large arbor fly reel for saltwater surf fishing is that of more rapid line retrieval. An example of where this is advantageous is when a speedy fish like any of the small tunas decides to make a run reversal and make a beeline right at the angler. Gathering line at a time like that is critical to maintaining contact with the fish and keeping tight with the hook. Of the various arbor sizes—standard, mid, large, and supersize—the most practical for the surf is the large arbor spool. Extra spools are a great way to increase the flexibility of a reel. Load the spools with different lines for fishing different conditions and you need only swap out spools, as conditions warrant.

Today's fly reels come in many sizes to meet the needs of fly anglers.

A strong and dependable drag is indispensable for surf fishing. The drag need not be capable of stopping a freight train, but it should pack enough wallop to slow down the biggest specimens of the fish you most often pursue. Whether fly fishing for tarpon, big striped bass, small tunas, bonefish, permit, or any gamefish that will run off to the races, a reel with a dependable drag is a rod's perfect mate.

Large arbor reels are a great choice for surf fishing.

As a line retrieval apparatus, fly reels are offered with one of three line retrieval mechanisms: single action, multiplier action, and automatic. When fishing the surf, keep it simple and choose a single action reel. It has less moving parts and is less prone to failure. Both multiplier and automatic reels have more complex mechanisms that salt water can wreak havoc on. Combine the benefits of large arbor and single action and you are good to go.

Fly Lines

Once upon a time, long, long ago, selecting a fly line was one of the most confusing aspects of fly fishing. Older silk lines were classified as level, double taper, or weight-forward, and also coded alphabetically for each of the respective line weights. Before you could buy a line, one literally had to decipher the unique coding. Fortunately for modern anglers the world of fly-line selection has gotten a lot easier. Fundamentally, there are three classifications of fly lines that are of interest to the saltwater surf angler: floating, sink-tip, and high-density sinking lines. While there are still a number of tapers to choose from, the most popular for salt water are those designed with a weight-forward taper. There are also a number of lines of interest that have been designed species-specific to better handle the conditions under which those fish are caught: bonefish taper, tarpon taper, a striper or little tunny line, etc. A weight-forward line is preferred in salt water because all the line weight is contained in a "belly" that is forward of the running line. That form of line taper is beneficial when quick rod loading and quick casts are required, and when confronted with

Fly lines are available to fish every level of the water column.

wind conditions. Weight-forward lines also offer an advantage when casting larger flies, as often is the case in saltwater surf fishing.

LINE DENSITY

Three types of fundamental lines densities are of importance to the surf fly angler: floating, sink tips, and full sinking. Floating lines are fully buoyant and are best used when fishing top water flies and poppers, or when fishing shallow water where longer lines and finer presentations are required, as with thin water tailing bonefish, redfish, or striped bass.

Sink tips come in an assortment of densities or weights that are designed to descend in the water column at varying sink rates: slow, intermediate, and fast. The line weights are classified in terms of grains as well as in sink rate in inches per second. Total tip weight is a function of the weight of the core material and the overall length of the tip. Tips can range in length from about five feet to more than thirty feet. Each rate of descent has application to different surf-fishing conditions. I've grown partial to three tip classifications that have become the heart of my surf-fishing line arsenal. The first is a high-density, fifteen-foot sink tip with a descent rate of about 2½ to 3½ inches per second. In stronger currents, I will often use a tip of similar length, but with a faster sink rate of 3¾ to 5½ inches per second.

A second sink tip that is of value in surf fishing is the intermediate clear tip. This is a favorite of mine for a number of reasons. The slow sink rate makes this tip ideal for fishing within the surf's wash, along the shoreline edge, or in quieter back bay areas and flats. This tip style can be used as an alternative to a floating line for fish in skinny water; the slow sink rate and the clear tip is a very effective combination. The clear intermediate tip works especially well for fish mudding for crustaceans or for those fish cruising the flats in search of a meal. One of the benefits of a clear tip is that the tip section can also perform double duty as a butt extension of the leader. Since the leader tip is clear, you can use a shorter tapered leader or just a straight length of leader tippet. I've often just used four to six feet of straight leader, even with fish like small tuna that have great eyesight, with no ill effects.

The last class of tips important to the surf angler are long-length, very high density tips that sink deep into the water column. Some of the very first of these lines to hit the line market were the creations of Jim Teeny. The lines became known simply by their originator's name: Teeny Lines or Teenies. Since then other manufacturers have added similar lines to their product offerings like Cortland's Quick Descent series of lines. The lines were originally designed for steelhead and salmon fishing but were embraced by the saltwater flyfishing community for fishing deep in the water column. My first exposure to Teeny sink tips was in Alaska for Pacific salmon. It was often said back then that if you wanted to catch Alaskan salmon consistently with a fly rod, you needed to learn to cast a Teeny line. These very heavy lines require a change in casting style due to their weight and the fact that you can't efficiently keep all of the line in the air for very long during the casting stroke. The stroke becomes more of a lob than a tight-loop cast. But learning the technique pays handsome dividends for the saltwater fly angler. These high-grain lines can help get a fly into the strike zone when fish are either lying close to the bottom or suspended in deep water.

While the previous tip configurations are integrated into the running line, shooting heads are yet another alternative for easily adapting to varying fishing conditions. The "heads" can be switched as needed and attached via loop-to-loop connections. A set of shooting heads, each of different weight, is a practical way to achieve effective depth management.

Leaders and Knots

For the most part, long tapered leaders are not necessary when fishing the surf. Short, four through eight feet lengths of fluorocarbon are all that one needs as a leader. A length of six feet is ideal. Fluorocarbon is a material that is more abrasion-resistant than monofilament leaders, and is virtually invisible when submerged. Another consideration in the case for short leaders is that many of the currently available lines come with clear tips that can fundamentally function as an alternative butt section for the tippet. This allows for shorter leaders to be employed. For most moderate-sized gamefish species, tippets of between a twelve and twenty pound test will more than suffice. For toothy critters like large bluefish, the addition of a short bite tippet of heavier strength pound-test is advisable.

Fluorocarbon is an excellent leader material for surf and wade fly fishing.

With regard to knots, there are a number of suitable connections that are effective for surf fly fishing, and many digital animations for tying those knots. In my experience I've developed a preference for the following: a nail knot or loop-to-loop connection for attaching the backing to the fly line and the fly line to the butt section of the leader; a blood knot or double uni-knot for building the leader; and a nonslip loop knot for attaching the fly to the leader.

Tie-able bite tippet material works well for toothy gamefish.

Chapter Two

Surf Scenarios

As indicated in the Introduction, surf fishing has been defined in its broadest sense to embrace all forms of wadable salt water. Each specific setting presents its own opportunities and challenges for the salty fly angler, and each often requires different techniques or strategies to maximize the fishing experience. While fishing similarities exist between the various types of locations, they each have unique characteristics that anglers must understand in order to enjoy successful fly fishing.

Beaches and the Surf Zone

Anglers fishing Eastern Seaboard and Southeast beaches will eventually encounter three types of primary beach venues: ocean-facing, sound-facing, and gulf-facing beaches. The sheer vastness of certain beaches often has both novice and sometimes seasoned anglers asking the inevitable, "Where do I start?" Over the years I have watched many surf anglers park their cars in a lot, walk a straight line down to the edge of the beach, and begin casting. I often wonder if they believe the fish will simply be there waiting for them? Oddly, sometimes the fish are, and I suspect that is what drives those same anglers to more of that specific behavior, preventing them from venturing out beyond their comfort zone. But there are also those anglers who are a bit more cerebral about where to enter the water and when to begin casting. I've watched them, too. Those anglers will almost never make a cast until they have had an opportunity to first survey the landscape and digest what they've seen. They will often look up and down the beach and then out at the water for any subtle signs of where fish might reside before choosing a direction to walk. Those meaningful subtleties can include: nervous water indicative of bait; bird activity that zeroes in on feeding fish; currents, rips, or eddies; visible structure such as jetties, outcroppings, groins, fingers of land, sand bars, and any type of break or alteration in the shoreline that might function to hold and attract baitfish. Granted, some anglers may be quite familiar with the stretches of beach they fish, but one reality of ocean-facing beaches is that they constantly change at the whim of winds, tide, and severe weather.

What may have been an intimate segment of beach one season might just become unfamiliar terrain the next. Hurricanes and nor'easters can wreak havoc on a beach and totally change and reorient sand, sand bars, and other forms of structure. I've witnessed the destructive power of strong nor'easters and hurricanes actually undermine stone structures to the point where the configuration was changed so dramatically that it no longer attracted or held fish. That scenario highlights why it is important for a surf-fly angler to continually learn about the beach he or she fishes— throughout the season and over the years.

The gradient of a beach or its slope is another critical factor in understanding and reading beach conditions that are conducive to effective fishing. Generally, the angle of grade will be in one of three forms: slight, moderate, or steep. Each of those conditions will impact the subsurface terrain and directly affect how one fishes the beach. While wind and wave action work in concert to continually transform the shoreline—redefining sand bars and troughs—the basic slope of a beach will shape what occurs close to the beach and beneath the water. An example of that takes place with shallow or moderate trenches or depressions that one often finds close to the merging of land and sea.

The land itself offers some of the best clues to what takes place beyond the shoreline. If the adjoining terrain is flat with little or no slope, that will usually signify a level

Typical stretch of Northeast beach.

Angle of grade on a beach or adjoining land can offer clues to the slope of the bottom beneath the water.

or flat entry into the water with slight depth variation for some distance out. Likewise, a gentle grade will most often indicate slight or moderate depth variation once one steps from shoreline and into the water. Lastly, cliffs, dunes, or other configurations of land with steep declines, like those formed by receding glaciers, will almost always indicate a sharp drop-off near to the shoreline. Some beaches with this characteristic can literally cause a drop from the shoreline of multiple feet, often just inches from the sand.

Each of the aforementioned conditions will influence the nature of the flyfishing experience. In situations where there is no slope or just a modest angle—combining with shallow water—fish might frequent those areas primarily in pre-dawn or after dark hours, when bait tends to move into those locations with a higher degree of comfort regarding their safety. The flatness of the contour might also require the angler to carefully wade greater distances to find small structural differences in the bottom. When confronted with flat bottoms, even the slightest variations can mean the difference between fish and no fish.

That said, there are also times when that flatness of contour might just attract fish from deeper water, especially when they are on the prowl for food. I have experienced situations along flat expanses of beach where an elbow or a J-bend forms; fish will move in close to corral bait along those areas. Moving down the slope ladder, the steep drop is a favorite of many surf fly anglers, especially if an adjoining sand bar or trough can be located. Under the best circumstances that configuration of shoreline variables will become a fish magnet. I have fished those types of conditions in the Northeast and Southeast, and in some instances fish were traveling the near shore trough just feet from my casting position.

Montauk Point is an example of multiple forms of structure merging.

One of the most notable places to surf fish in the entire world is Montauk, New York. While it is a productive surf venue throughout the entire fishing season, it is an extraordinary place to fish in the fall during the mass migration of striped bass, little tunny, and bluefish. When one witnesses the annual spectacle it becomes easy to understand why this section of surf is so productive. The Montauk Point promontory is the easternmost point of Long Island and New York. It juts out into the Atlantic Ocean and sits between two large expanses of sand beaches found on its north and south sides. The core beach area directly off The Point is strewn with rocks and boulders, replete with rips, tidal currents, and eddies. In essence, Montauk Point is an example of super structure comprised of many elements, all of which work in concert to attract masses of bait and gamefish. Montauk is the archetype for the ideal surf-fishing location, and the most important lesson it teaches the surf fly angler is that multiple forms of shoreline structure in any given location are always better than one form.

Inlets and Passes

Natural and manmade inlets and passes dot the entire length of the eastern seaboard, both along the Atlantic ocean and on the Gulf. Regardless of how these formations were created, they attract and hold fish throughout the seasons. Inlets and passes also function as portals from one habitat form to another. In the Northeast, for example, an inlet is a transition point for fish moving from back bay areas out into the Atlantic Ocean. In the Southeast, a pass will allow fish to move from the backcountry or a sound into the ocean or the Gulf. In general terms, inlets separate larger open bodies of water from smaller contained areas. The narrow configuration of an inlet generates significant current during changes in tidal phase, making these areas productive fishing locations. Similarly, a pass is a gouge or cut between two land formations that result in water flows like those of inlets, which funnel moving water at an accelerated rate.

Both inlets and passes present challenging but interesting opportunities for the shore-bound fly angler. While most such formations are often best fished from a boat, there are many occasions when the wading angler will have an advantage. First and foremost, all such areas by way of design create points at either end of the land masses that form the inlets or passes. These locations are typically wadable, but that must be done with caution as currents can be very strong. Due to the fast-moving flows, baitfish and other forms of food sources will often tumble about in a manner that attracts gamefish to an easy meal. When those currents intersect with either land-based structure such as rocks, bends in land contour, sand bars, and troughs, fish will often lie in wait in and around that structure for bait to be brought to them. Fish will also take up residence in the eddies, pools, and calmer water that exits around the down current sides of the inlet or pass. Sand beaches that run perpendicular to the terminal points of outflows can be very productive since fish will hold along those sorts of areas. Any structure that exists on the inside portions of the inlet or pass, like a sand or gravel flat, is also a potential area of opportunity. In those situations where strong currents move around inlet points, deeper water can be often found as a result of the gouging effect of the fast moving water. Troughs or depressions in the bottom contour can be formed in this manner. Larger fish will often frequent these deeper inlet or pass locations.

Areas on either side of an inlet can be productive locations to prospect.

Flats

A flat is fundamentally a large expanse of very shallow or thin water used by gamefish as a cruising plateau, a formation where they can hunt or root out food and then escape to a deeper safe haven. This type of water can be ankle-deep or range to a few feet in depth, and it is usually also associated with sight fishing, the process of casting to fish one actually sees. Sand flats are ideal configurations for the wading fly angler. A flat more often than not affords access to deeper water; fish move up onto the flat to feed and then exit to the security of the surrounding depths. The deep-water access is also used for defensive purposes. Since most fish sense vulnerability when feeding on a flat, a residual imprint from when they were fry, the security of an escape route is an essential feature of productive flats. Fishing flats are not only unique to the Southeast and tropical locales. Similar conditions and structures do exist throughout the Northeast, and a number of enterprising captains, guides, and anglers have explored and developed that potential for quite some time, opening up an entirely new world of flats fishing to regions beyond traditional Southeast and Gulf Coast locations.

Flats can be quite large, as in miles long, or they can be much smaller and on a scale of but fifty to 100 yards in length. Some favorite Northeast flats that I have fished are quite small and don't hold legions of fish, yet they can be productive during certain times of the day, periods of the tide, and seasons. Classic flats fishing

Typical Northeastern flat. (Photo credit: Laura Pisano)

is most always identified with tropical or southerly locations and with places like Florida, the Yucatan, Belize, and the Bahamas. One of the key elements for flats-style fishing is crystal clear water. You need to see the fish to which you are casting. Sunny days are a critical factor since they enhance the angler's ability to spot the often difficult-to-discern forms of cruising or stationary fish. The combination of bright, sunny days and the ephemeral images of fish make polarized sunglasses an essential piece of equipment.

The entire range of the Southeast is filled with flats fishing opportunities. The Northeast coast also has significant potential for this form of fishing. One can find suitable areas to sight fish from Atlantic City, New Jersey to the bays and tidal river mouths of Maine. The fact of the matter is that most of the Northeast still has areas that are waiting to be explored.

While many flats can be accessed by direct wading, others may require the use of either a flats boat or a conveyance like a kayak. Those crafts can be used to get the angler to the flat where wade fishing techniques can then be employed. Stealth is a critical element of successful flats fishing, and wade fishing allows for a quiet and furtive approach. The best flats fly anglers will always approach a flat cautiously, quietly, and alert. A typical tactic is to first work the peripheral edges of the flat. Fish will habitually cruise that seam area between the shallow water of the flat and the deeper

An expansive Southeastern flat.

perimeter water. Once on the flat, the angler can slowly wade to areas where fish are known to concentrate or can be observed feeding. Exposed tails, fins, and "mud" patches are signs of rooting and feeding activity.

Tidal movements make a big difference. Fish will locate on different portions of a flat during the various tide phases. Low levels of water are always ideal for the wading angler. When fishing a flat for the first few times, it is beneficial to work the area as thoroughly as possible in some orderly pattern since you never know where you might bump some bass. When fish-holding areas are located, such as pot-holes, grass, or mussel beds, or changes in the bottom contours and structure, the angler can move about slowly to thoroughly prospect the location. You also want to keep noise to a minimum since those reverberations will send fish fleeing in a heartbeat.

The ability to spot fish on a flat in time to make an effective presentation of a fly is the most critical element of this game. All too often the untrained eye misses the camouflaged form that is either moving along the flat or just feet from the boat. This makes the use of polarized sunglasses essential. Learn how to spot not only the entire fish form but also pieces and parts of the whole. Feeding fish will usually travel about the flat searching out a meal or remain positioned in a feeding lane waiting for food to come to them. Striped bass especially will often feed this way and orient to a favored holding area. I have watched stripers root sand eels at dusk in the same

Sand and mud flat.

manner that redfish or bonefish will root out small crustaceans and crabs. If the water is skinny enough, you will see the backs and exposed tails of feeding fish. When that happens, try to maintain your composure, use stealth, and make the casts count!

When wading a flat always exercise caution. It is often best to take small steps and shuffle one's feet as you move along. This can help avoid an unpleasant encounter with nasty critters like sting rays. It also helps to pay constant attention to your surroundings. While flats are generally shallow situations, large fish will often move onto a flat to feed. I once was startled by a rather large bull shark while wading and fortunately made it back to the skiff without incident. The angler also needs to pay attention to tides. One can often loose track of increasing water levels that can rise quickly and strand an angler.

Harbors, Bays, Back Bays, and Backcountry

Harbors are typically associated with safe havens where any variety of water craft can seek shelter from inclement weather, and are places where boats are moored when not in use. Harbors are either crafted by nature or manmade. Those made with human intervention have a lot more engineering involved with the designs, typically will include such structures as jetties and sea walls, and will often have been dredged to accommodate larger vessels. Not only do those engineered harbor attributes intentionally create a safe environment, but unintentionally also create a habitat suitable for gamefish. I am always amazed at how many boating anglers simply blast out from harbors without at least stopping to fish some of the most productive structures

Back waters offer some of the best wade fishing surprises.   (Photo credit: Rich Santos)

they will encounter throughout the entire day on the water. Harbors can be a bonanza for the wading angler.

One consistent characteristic of manmade harbors is the presence of jetties that form the entrance. Unequivocally, all jetties attract and hold baitfish and gamefish. For the fly angler on foot this creates many seasonal opportunities. The heads and tails of jetties will often offer some of the most productive fishing along the structure. Those locations will always generate currents, and depending on wind, waves, and tide, one side might be more productive than the other. One of the hottest jetty spots to fish is an adjoining beach or shoreline that abuts the jetty. That is a place where bait will congregate and, therefore, will almost always draw predatory game species.

Although the tips of jetties are classic honey holes, the wise angler will explore the entire length of a jetty. Nooks, crevices, and crannies will invite all sorts of creatures including the fish that feed on them. Deep water channels will also be within reach of the fly angler and fish will migrate through those thoroughfares It can not be emphasized enough that anglers who fish jetties should do so with the utmost of caution. Jetties can be very dangerous. Fishermen are often swept off jetty rocks by large waves, slip into the water, or fall between boulder cracks. When fishing a jetty always wear some form of metal cleats over your boots. There are a number of very suitable products on the market from fishing and climbing boot manufacturers. When fly fishing from a jetty I like to carry two different fly lines: an intermediate sink tip and either a high-grain sink tip or a full sinking. Fish that are near jetties will often be caught in the lower levels of the water column; weighted flies can prove especially effective in the currents and depths around jetties.

Once inside a harbor, other wading opportunities can be found. Many large harbors may also contain coves, marshes, grass expanses, sod banks, small islands, and drains. Each of those features provides plentiful wading opportunities for the surf fly angler. Find a few forms of structure that interconnect and interrelate and you might uncover some terrific fly fishing. One of the harbors I fly fish on foot in the Northeast contains all the elements mentioned, and while the fishing is far from easy, it can be rewarding on a consistent basis. In that setting I've enjoyed days catching fish off the open beach adjacent to the jetty, from the jetty, from sand bars inside the harbor, from a small sand flat, and from a sod bank. All fishing was done with an intermediate sink tip and a small assortment of baitfish and crustacean flies to match the prevalent bait. In addition, harbors provide docking facilities and those structures attract and hold fish. And all one needs do is walk the docks and make prospecting casts to likely looking holding areas. Docks are especially productive at night. In the Southeast it is one of the most effective ways to catch snook. The dock lights attract and retain baitfish, and inevitably snook will follow. The same approach works well in the Northeast for striped bass. When feeding in this manner fish are quite receptive to flies.

Natural harbors have the same potential for excellent structure and fish catching opportunities. Those formations differ from manmade harbors in that Mother Nature framed her creations with borders of natural land. In situations where the water is of sufficient depth inside the harbor, the formation can be used for purposes of mooring and anchorage. Natural harbors typically offer a variety of shoreline flyfishing opportunities as well as ample backwater formations like sand and grass flats, sod banks, lagoons, and coves.

Back bays and backcountry are other natural formations that provide a wealth of flyfishing opportunities for wading anglers. Those locations too are rife with structural fish magnets like islands, mangroves, grass fields, lagoons, coves, shorelines, sod banks, flats, and every other type of structure previously discussed. Primary bays can be large bodies of water like Maine's Saco Bay, Massachusetts's Cape Cod Bay, New York's Great South Bay, Maryland's Chesapeake Bay, and Florida's Whitewater Bay. While most of these formations are often best fished via watercrafts and boats, kayaks and other small crafts can be used to get the angler to wadable areas. Back bay and backcountry areas can also be contained within the larger bays or as part of large harbors. Regardless of location, these backwater situations often host very fer-

Nice redfish taken from remote back water area.   (Photo credit: Rich Santos)

tile fisheries that can be active throughout the seasons. The spring and early summer seasons can often be prime times to wade and cast flies.

Jetties

While jetty-type configurations have been discussed previously in the context of being a part of other forms of structure, jetties are also of importance to fly anglers on foot. All jetties attract marine life, yet not all segments of the jetty are equally productive. Variations in jetty construction and the placement of large stones or stone blocks will create a substructure within the formation where bait can hide and where predatory gamefish will lie in wait to ambush prey. Fish will also move up and down the length of a jetty as tidal movements change and as currents form. When fishing jetties I always observe bait and larger fish darting about areas adjacent to the stacked rocks. Typically those rocks are stacked in a manner that forms a wide base that narrows toward the top. In the context of fly fishing the surf, jetties are most relevant as entrances to harbors, boundaries along passes, and bordering inlets that lead from the ocean or gulf to back bays and backcountry areas. Jetties are also used to manage water flow at both the outlets of the rivers, places where fish will often congregate.

For maximum results a jetty should be fished thoroughly: front to back, either side, and all levels of the water column. While fan-casting the tip of a jetty can

All jetties attract and hold baitfish that, in turn, attract gamefish.

be very productive, any areas where currents have, over time, cut deep holes and troughs should be prospected as well. Intermediate and high density sink tips, as well as full sinking lines, will cover all situations encountered when fly casting from a jetty. An assortment of flies that match to prevalent bait that inhabit areas in and around the jetty will work well. Include heavily weighted patterns that can be used to dredge near bottom areas where gamefish will often hold or move through.

The fly angler should negotiate a jetty with the utmost caution. Jetties can be dangerous places to fish. The rocks are often slick with algae or moss. Creases, cracks, and crevices in the rocks make for perilous footing, and a rogue wave can easily sweep an angler from a position atop a jetty. Always wear some form a spiked boot or over-boot to help maintain footing.

River Outlets, Tidal Creeks, and Tidal Ponds

Gamefish are drawn naturally to river mouths, river outlets, and tidal creeks, and with good reason: these are places where bait will congregate and where currents consistently form. Points where these formations meet other bodies of water or where there is a confluence of currents are often the most productive places to cast flies. Access to river mouths and tidal creeks is generally "friendly" for wading anglers. Small boats or kayaks can also be used for greater flexibility and for searching deeper into areas like tidal creeks. Fly fishing the points of outflow are often the most challenging and rewarding, especially when gamefish seasonally transition to those areas. River outlets can be excellent areas to fish when anadromous species like striped bass or shad amass in those locations prior to seasonally moving from salt water to fresh water and then back again.

Areas where flows come together and currents mingle should always be fished, especially pools, eddies, and seam water. Very often there are areas of flats in and around these structures that form on the inside of

Southeastern backwater creek. (Photo credit: Nick Angelo)

the current flows. Carefully waded, these flats can offer productive fishing when gamefish move up onto the shallows to cruise and feed.

Water coming out from a river or tidal creek will flow in a manner that will often create secondary forms of structures

Tidal creek at low tide.

like channels and troughs. These formations will take shape depending upon the direction bias and speed of the current. Regardless of those considerations, structures of that sort should always be fished if one can safely negotiate the terrain.

One of the joys of fly fishing these types of areas is that they can be fished in classic fashion with up-current quartering casts, mending line to drift flies naturally

Creek fishing for striped bass.   (Photo credit: Vincent Catalano)

to laid up fish or those that may be in feeding lanes, seam water or reverse eddies, and pools. Sinking tips or full sinking lines work best under these conditions, but a slow sinking intermediate tip will get the job done for the flats.

Much of what has been discussed thus far regarding river outlets and tidal creeks pertains as well to tidal ponds. One such prototypical pond is within the boundaries of my home fishing waters in the Northeast. It often holds large quantities of bait and attracts many varied gamefish species during the prime seasons. Current flows are dependent on tidal phase and resulting water movement. As the tide moves toward flood stage and the pond fills, bait and gamefish will gather inside. When the tide shifts toward low water, fish will retreat from the pond and move back into a larger body of water. Some fish will often remain until extreme low water and feed on sand and mud flats that have formed inside the pond. In the Northeast this occurs most often in the spring and early summer months. In more southerly climates, ponds of this sort can remain productive throughout the year. In an area with a quick tide turnaround, large tidal ponds will rarely empty completely. Outward water flow will often continue as the incoming tidal bulge occurs. This merging of opposing water forces will create rip currents, the fringes of which become hot spots for fish. I've fished a pond where this occurrence takes place and having the ability to wade within casting distance of the rip current will often yield fish.

Tidal ponds fill and empty with water and bait.

Water flows that emanate outward from ponds are very river-like and create many of the same structural formations at the outlet, as are prominent with rivers and tidal creeks.

Sounds and Estuaries

Whether fishing the Vineyard Sound, Long Island Sound, Currituck Sound, or Pine Island Sound, sounds and estuaries are often home to very fertile fisheries. A sound is a fiord-like, expansive body of water that is deeper than a bay or lagoon and connects one land mass to another. It is also separated from a larger ocean or gulf by a section or strip of land. It is usually somewhat sheltered and is affected by tidal movements. A sound is often open at either one or both ends.

An estuary is a body of salt water into which fresh water flows from connecting rivers and streams. This mixing of fresh and salt water creates a nourishing environment that often functions as nursery for juvenile fish species. Estuaries are complex ecosystems and some bodies of water like the Long Island Sound are actually both an estuary and a sound, formations that are highly productive fishing areas.

Whether fishing an estuary or a sound, the fly angler will often encounter most, if not all, the previously discussed forms of structure. Those structures will often be available to anglers on foot or to those using watercrafts to access wading areas.

A sound is situated between two bodies of land and are productive ecosystems and estuaries.

Chapter Three

Increase Your Surf IQ

The elite quarterbacks in the NFL have an uncanny ability to read defenses. They are capable of understanding and predicting what defensive alignments are about to be employed as the next play unfolds. Some of that aptitude is innate, sort of an instinctive sixth sense, but much of a quarterback's reaction is the result of learned behaviors. Top-tier professional QBs can read and anticipate the moves of linebackers, cornerbacks, and safeties. They often change the offensive play based on what they see and sense. In essence, they can view the entire landscape of the playing field and transform that vision into a successful play. The same can be said of good surf fly anglers who can read water and understand what is going on beneath the surface. As an angler increases his or her ability to assimilate, comprehend, and apply knowledge to the fishing scene, the odds of successful outings rise.

Observe and Learn

The given reality of surf fishing East Coast waters in the Age of the Internet is that there are no longer many secret spots—just spots that hold their secrets. Unlocking those mysteries can become a lifelong mission for the ardent fly angler, especially those who target fish in the wash and with the long rod. There are no short cuts to this process, and the best fishermen I know spend as much time learning to read water and understanding the gamefish they pursue as they do with the actual fishing. Some surf anglers might choose to take a path of least resistance and simply follow the lead of others, but earning one's stripes is the only way to achieve consistent results and a more thorough understanding of the variables that affect one's angling success. Modeling your own fishing after how successful anglers catch fish is certainly a beneficial and acceptable tactic, and it surely cuts down on the learning curve; but unless one learns the reasons why fish bite and why they don't, the game is far less intriguing and rewarding. Fly fishing, after all is said and done, is a sport that involves a continuing process of discovery. Good surf anglers make it a point to learn

Take notes of your scouting and check maps for a heads-up on new spots.

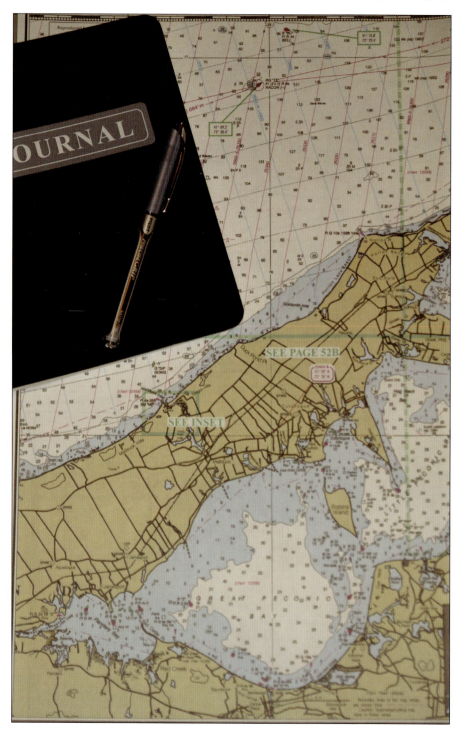

something new each time they are on the water, whether they catch fish or not. Even dreaded "skunk" days teach volumes about fishing. Listening to nature speak and being constantly observant are as essential to success as the fly you tie onto the end of your line. A very successful captain and flyfishing guide once told me that when it comes to fishing, "preparation plus observation equals success." My own experiences have taught me that those words of wisdom represent sound advice.

A Case Study

While fly fishing with a friend a couple of seasons back I couldn't help but take notice as he meticulously prospected a small section of beach, intent on finding some clues to striped bass eating habits during the waning phase of an outgoing tide. I fished with flies while he cast artificial plugs. He was dogged in his pursuit as he waded into rough surf, climbed rocks, scaled jetties like a Billy Goat, changed plugs, and studiously observed water conditions until he hit upon the right combination of variables. Eventually his perseverance paid off with a nice bass. But what absolutely amazed me was what happened after he hooked and landed several consecutive quality stripers. A squadron of pick-up trucks materialized out of nowhere, doors swung open, coffee cups and donuts went flying all over the parking area as a legion of surfcasters scrambled to gather their gear and cash in on the find. One such member of the invasion force that I nicknamed on the spot "William Tell" was shouting instructions to all who would listen, "The fish are coming, the fish are coming." And one poor soul didn't even waste time putting on his waders. He just marched into

Secluded spots offer the wading angler some of the most enjoyable fly fishing.
(Photo credit: Rich Santos)

the cold suds in his leisure suit, casting wildly! This scene was somewhat more reminiscent of *One Flew Over the Cuckoos Nest* than an unfolding fishing drama. While all the newcomers were welcomed to the scene I couldn't help but think that, had more of their time been spent fishing, searching, and learning, rather than chomping on glazed baked goods, perhaps some enlightening fish secrets would have been revealed to them as well.

As it turned out that piece of beach got crowded very fast, so my friend and I decided to leave the surfside chaos behind and take a long walk farther down the sand. Fishing the same "patterns" that had just previously proven successful, we continued to catch bass for most of the remaining tide, and each time we happened upon similar configurations of structure, currents, and bait. And best of all, we were able to find our own little slice of seclusion away from now growing crowds. In my book, the fish you find and catch on your own are the most gratifying.

Reading and Interpreting Water

One angling certainty is that fish are not always intent on committing suicide by hooking themselves. While surface explosions of baitfish and gamefish are the makings of very visual and often frantic angling experiences, those occasions are not the everyday norm. If you are around water long enough you can surely expect to encounter this kind of action throughout the seasons. While it is true that even a blind squirrel finds nuts occasionally, you can't be betting your long-term beach fishing success on happenstance encounters with these surface feeding scenarios. To be consistently successful at "catching" fish in the surf throughout the entire year, avid fly anglers must learn to find fish when they aren't visibly showing; that is usually about 95 percent of the time. This is when an aptitude for reading the characteristics of water

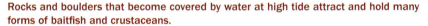
Rocks and boulders that become covered by water at high tide attract and hold many forms of baitfish and crustaceans.

Multiple forms of back-bay structure will hold fish at high water.

Find an old shipwreck and it will most likely hold bait and fish.   (Photo credit: Rich Santos)

Combinations of structures are often the most productive.

Structures like sunken barges near shore are also worth exploring.

and understanding structure pay huge dividends. Comprehending and applying the relationships between fish, bait, and structure are essential to surf-fishing success.

Critical surf-related structures come in many forms, such as jetties, rock piles, reefs, sand flats, gravel flats, oyster beds, shallow troughs, pot holes, etc. The time spent learning the intricacies of that structure is priceless, as is the knowledge one gains studying the feeding and migration habits of bait and gamefish. There is an old freshwater fishing adage that 90 percent of the fish are in 10 percent of the available water. That maxim is true in salt water as well. But the 10 percent in the brine is constantly subject to change. A certain stretch of beach or waterway can be much more productive than other sections in the same general area. And, depending upon the influences of wind, weather, waves, and the seasonal whims of Mother Nature, these productive locations can change dramatically from one year to the next. While we may look out upon the vast and inviting expanse of green or blue, it all is not a prolific sea, and therein lies the challenge that draws us to this sport.

Surf fly anglers especially enjoy the thrill of the chase. They arm themselves with casting tools that require a bit more skill and practice to operate efficiently than do other forms of fishing apparatus.

Boulder fields and striped bass are a perfect match. (Photo credit: Laura Pisano)

They sometimes assemble their own baits from an assortment of plastic, metal, fur, feathers, and synthetic materials, and then wade forth with high hopes of employing trickery to outwit fish that often times seem more intelligent than we are . . . and we love it! For most of the surf flyfishing crowd, the greatest joy of this form of angling is actually finding the fish and getting them to strike. For some, the actual catching is secondary!

Eyes Wide Open

My own epiphany occurred while walking a local beach a number of years ago. It was during the neap tides of early spring and I wasn't actually fishing but rather walking and jogging for exercise. Yet even though I had no rod in hand, my mind was doing its own fishing of sorts, scanning the terrain and the water as I jogged. At one point I was instantly stopped in my tracks by something I'd seen in the crystal clear water about forty yards off the beach. I had caught a lot of fish in the vicinity of the point upon which my eyes were now locked but I had never quite figured out the reasons why. Fly fishing from the beach and my boat often brought success in this general area. I backed away from the water's edge and climbed to a higher vantage point for a better look at this seemingly new discovery. There to my amazement was a sand bar, a trough, and a series of boulders all arranged in such a way as I had never noticed before. The specific alignment of this combined structure created a conduit that generated a substantial current.

Survey landscapes from a high vantage point during low water tide phases.

As I watched the remaining outward movement of the tide, it became apparent that this location was productive due to accelerating water that flowed through the area. The ensuing current would most certainly tumble bait about, creating whirlpools and reverse eddies filled with hapless prey. My elevated perspective, combined with an extreme low tide and the movement of water, gave me a much clearer picture of the dynamics of a productive fishing hole; insight to a spot that I had never before recognized either from the beach or boat. It now became quite apparent why various species of gamefish would regularly frequent this area.

Building on that experience my beach fishing successes in that area increased as I located other similar configurations where fish behaviors and structure patterns would also be somewhat predictable. I now always wade about the beach with eyes wide open.

Stop, Look, and Listen

I had another similar experience while fishing alone just a few years ago. For the longest time I had taken my boat to one particular spot, always anticipating fish. The area had all the ear markings of a potential hot spot, but I visited that location for three consecutive years without so much as a single bite. I just couldn't figure out the location's secret and it had become a personal challenge to do so. But on one occasion, approaching the area on foot, I noticed literally hundreds of fiddler crabs scurrying about on the wet sand. I watched as the fleeing crabs made their way from a small tidal flat into their burrows. A few were swept away into more rapidly moving currents. I chose this spot as my point of entry. I waited and I watched and I finally heard that familiar pop of a feeding bass. A favorite early season hybrid crab pattern was tied to my leader as I made a cast that would position my fly to drift along

Drift crab patterns through areas where crustaceans are present.

with the natural bait. As the fake crustacean swung in the current and disappeared, the line immediately went tight. I strip set the hook and soon thereafter landed a nice school bass, the first from that spot in all those years of trying. Subsequent casts brought similar results. I visited that spot for three more days, catching and releasing more than a hundred bass, mostly larger-sized school bass but also a few keeper-sized fish as well. What was most revealing to me was that the window of opportunity for catching these bass was a brief period of about forty–five minutes. Before and after that I couldn't catch a striper if my life depended on it. I then visited that spot with my boat during the same portion of the tide cycle and positioned it in such a way as to attempt the same exact presentation of the fly. It didn't work! Only wading that spot produced results. Why? Because the angle of fly presentation from land combined with an outgoing tidal flow and resulting current created the most realistic drift of the fly.

But another revealing fact was that once my wading excursions no longer re-sulted in observing that precise crab behavior, the fishing ceased. Eventually, I no longer caught bass there. It became obvious that the key was the ideal convergence of preferred bait plus an optimal stage of the tide, some unique structure, and a critical fly presentation. All this I would have never figured out had I not walked and waded that spot.

Other similar wading discoveries have included finding pot holes, troughs, drop-offs, and subtle depressions off the beach that also hold fish during certain tide phases, faint tide lines, and unique areas of current movement.

Valuable Lessons

The most valuable lesson I've learned from my surf-fishing experiences is to connect the dots. Just like the pro quarterback, it is essential for the surf angler to not only see the pieces of the puzzle but to understand the interrelationships and join to-gether all the variables. The connections between successful wade fishing and read-ing water are inexorably linked, especially for the angler who fishes intimately close to shore. Even those who venture farther from the beach can benefit from observing the patterns and habits of fish that move between deeper offshore haunts and inshore beach locations. The reverse is also often true; observations that you make while fish-ing from a boat can help with your beach fishing. Daily or seasonal migration habits will teach priceless lessons. I benefited from a situation like that a few years back dur-ing a very prolific run of Atlantic bonito. After a number of productive boat outings for the "bones," my engine had to be brought in for service during a peak period of the run. Not wanting to miss out on the exceptional action I took to the beach armed with the elements of my boat fishing success. As I waded the beach, that knowledge of the daily feeding routine of the bonito proved invaluable. Several bonito later, I

Releasing a surf-caught bonito.

knew that specific feeding patterns I had observed while boat fishing had served me
well when those learned lessons were applied to my beach fishing. Lessons are where
you find them. You just need to keep your mind open to the messages you are given.

Throughout the years I have come to know certain surf fly anglers who are very
good at consistently zeroing in on the fish. It is as if they have that extra sense, which
is a throwback to the days of our primal ancestors. These fishermen vigorously embrace the journey of discovery. Finding fish consistently is not always easy; it takes
time on the water and a lot of hard work. Yet, the results are always well worth the
efforts. Certain stretches of beach or waterway can be much more productive than
other sections in the same general area. And—as I have referenced before—the influences of nature upon productive locations can change fishing results dramatically
from one year to the next.

Chapter Four

Elements of Surf Structure

Edges, corners, and points of transition are attractors for all varieties of fish and game. Fishermen and hunters alike gravitate toward contour changes in pursuit of quarry that have a proclivity for these areas of structure. A big largemouth bass on an outer edge of a submerged brush pile, a huge buck in the corner of a woodlot, or striped bass at the transition point from sand to rocks along the beach are all examples of prime locations that wildlife and fish frequent. The salty-surf fly angler would be well served to pay attention to contour changes, topography transitions, and other similar geographic variations in structure. Learning to discover, read, and effectively fly-fish these areas will add immensely to surf-fishing success.

A Revealing Scenario

A few seasons back I was fly fishing a stretch of a favorite Long Island beach during the pre-dawn hours. It was early spring, prime time to encounter bass feeding on sand eels. Shuffling along the predominant sand bottom, cast after cast was made without a single striped bass showing so much as passing interest in the fly. At one point I sensed a bottom change through my wading boot; the structure beneath my feet transitioned from smooth, soft sand to what turned out to be a pebbly and stone-filled bottom. Within two or three subsequent lateral steps from that changeover, a stout striper struck the sand eel pattern. A few casts later, another bass hit. At the time I didn't think much of it and continued my way down the beach, moving off the rocky bottom and back onto sand. But after wading an additional 100 yards without another hit, I began thinking about the pebbles and stones that had been underfoot. Retracing my steps back to that general area of bottom change I re-positioned over the sand bottom and waded slowly, casting as I shuffled along. As fate or structure would have it, once I hit upon the pebbled bottom, yet another bass ate the fly. Coincidence? That proved not to be the case. Continuing along in this fashion, many more bass ate the sand eel fly. What now became obvious was that as long as I

A stretch of beach that transitioned from sand to a pebble bottom yielded this fine striped bass.

remained within the parameters of that small area of transition I caught bass. Moving off from that seemingly preferred bottom situation generated no other bite. It was as if bass were nonexistent.

Distance measured in feet literally defined the difference between success and failure. I continued to catch bass that morning as long as I stayed within the boundaries of the gravely transition zone. When the tide quit so did the bite. But what was more enlightening than the day's events was that this pattern of activity continued for more than a week of fishing, and for as long as I moved from one similar bottom configuration to another. Even more of a revelation was that this scenario also played out in similar fashion from one season to the next. If sand eels were in this zone, the areas of transition from sand bottom to pebbles would consistently yield fish.

More of the Same

As obvious as the previous structure transition was, other situations often prove to be a lot less evident and much more subtle. That is especially true when on a long sand beach or on a flat. Serendipity or happenstance may prove helpful to the salty-surf fly rodder if one keeps an open mind and is curious about conditions that produce fish and conditions that don't. Such was the situation during an early summer outing to another Northeast beach. The day was turning into more of an extended hike than a fishing trip. While I knew striped bass and bluefish were in the neighborhood, more than a mile of wading and casting had not surrendered a single fish. I knew it wasn't for lack of bait or choice of fly, since the generic pattern I had tied on was proven for replicating slim baitfish like the spearing and sand eels that were in the area. I caught fish earlier that week from my boat but this surf foray was coming up empty.

Moving onto a section of beach that turned back to form an indentation in the shoreline, I became much more deliberate and focused with my casting. I've learned over the years that any change in shoreline contour, regardless of how subtle, is worth prospecting. My efforts were not immediately rewarded. I had covered about forty yards of beach and had come up empty. Continuing to cast up-current with the outgoing tide, I moved slowly along the shoreline. Mending fly line allowed the fly to descend during its drift and move at a natural pace with the current. I would slowly take up line until the fly reached the end of the drift and then slowly strip the fly to life. It was precisely at that point when the first fish struck—at the end of the drift and as the fly moved toward the surface, prompted by a tightening line. It turned out to be a keeper-size striper. I continued to cast to that area for about a half hour and picked up a few more bass. Nothing seemed unusual about this spot but that it held fish. It wasn't until later on that day when the tide receded that I realized why.

Sand bars and sand fingers that run along a beach can be very productive locations to fly fish.   (Photo credit: Rich Santos)

Unknown to me at the time, I had been standing on a very understated point—hardly noticeable at the flood stage of the tide. When I returned to this location at the end of the outgoing flow I saw instantly why fish held there. The miniscule point of land reached out as a finger of sand into a channel that funneled out from a cluster of submerged boulders. There was a lot going on in that small area and it became instantly evident why the current moved the way it did, allowing my fly an almost ideal drift. The boulder configuration was such that it created a "venturi"-type effect of water, like that of carburetor jets. The opening in the boulders allowed the water to speed up and form a vortex that followed the edge of the sand bar. That proved to be an ideal situation for bait to get washed through and into the waiting mouths of bass and bluefish hanging on the edges of the current. The relevant point here is that the combination of a subtle point, a sand bar, and submerged boulders created a perfect mixture of structure that the fish oriented to. While I happened upon this combination of fish-attracting elements by chance, taking the time to understand the reasons it was productive paid off handsomely on all future trips.

Productive Structure Formations

Fish-attracting configurations can take many forms. For the salty fly rodder, beaches, bays, jetties, inlets, and backcountry areas offer a plethora of great places

Jetties create turbulence that tumbles bait about and attracts predatory gamefish.

to pursue and catch fish. The glacial movements that formed much of the Northeast coast left behind a wealth of sand, stones, rocks, boulders, and flats, all of which attract and hold bait and gamefish. The entire length of the Northeast coast has the most consistent and far-reaching boulder fields, since that coastal edge was the terminal point of the receding ice-age glaciers. Various types of rocky structure abound, very often in close proximity to the shore-bound angler. Yet, rock structures are not limited only to those of natural formations. Man-made riprap and jetties are classic forms of fish-attracting structure, and those can be found on both shores and in substantial numbers. An inlet or harbor typically opens to the ocean or sound through a jetty. These areas almost always maintain some degree of current that is like a magnet

Mud banks often yield quality fish.   (Photo credit: Alberto Knie)

Backwater grass banks and grass flats offer some of the finest wade fishing.
(Photo credit: Rich Santos)

Large boulders like these that are fully submerged during periods of high tide are best for attracting gamefish.

to gamefish. At certain times of the year, jetty formations can be the most productive structures to fish. They all attract bait and, therefore, gamefish. As an example, little tunny love jetties since bait gets tossed about in the turbulence and become easy pickings. Jetties are a perennial point of return for inshore pelagics.

Moving farther down the east coast, specifically in the Southeast and Florida, land was formed more as a result of volcanic activity and sedimentation. Limestone bedrock is at the core of these geologic formations. While glaciations at the end of the ice age had profound effects on the coastal configuration of the Northeast, sea level changes in the Southeast affected the formation of the limestone bedrock and the underwater landscape. Over thousands of years, the obvious impact of these changes have been "structural" alterations along inshore areas where fly anglers ply their trade.

Regardless of whether one fishes the Northeast or Southeast, points of land, land protrusions, and promontories that jut out into the water are very productive places to fish. Points combining with rocks, sand, and boulders are especially good spots to fly fish. One rule of thumb to follow is that multiple forms of structures blending together in an area are usually much better than any one single form. Structure also takes the form of grass, sand flats, or sod banks that merge into deeper water at a break line—the point where shallow water meets deep water.

Channels, cuts, ledges, and drop offs of any variation are always worth quality fishing time. Also, any convergence of currents that form a seam usually indicates something going on beneath the surface to cause that disparate movement of flows. I always toss a fly into seam water, and never pass up fishing it thoroughly. Learning to interpret what one sees on the surface of the water is fundamental to understanding what takes place beneath the surface. Top level water often behaves in ways that directly correlate to the influences of subsurface structure. Productive currents, eddies, and white water are all beneficial byproducts of often unseen turbulence.

All beaches are not created equal when it comes to holding fish. Some stretches are consistently more productive than others. Specific structure has a lot to do with those tendencies. Other beaches may be productive during certain seasons, stages of tide, or current flow. When fish are not in beach blitz mode, look for any variation from the norm. Ninety-five percent of one's beach flyfishing experience will be with fish that aren't visibly showing. An ability to read beach conditions is as important as technical fishing skill. Any change in beach contour or any formations that appear out of the ordinary are worth exploring. And don't just fish a spot once. Keep at it during different tide stages, at different times of the day, and during certain periods of the season. It always pays to prospect manmade structure such as bulkheads, bridges, and docks, as all varieties of fish will gravitate to those structures.

You just never know when a piece of beach structure might turn into a honey hole. Surf fly anglers need to be cognizant of changes to beach configurations that result from severe weather. Hurricanes and nor'easters can dramatically alter the contour of sand beaches and completely reorient structure like sand bars, flats, pot holes, areas around inlets, and mangrove islands.

Closer Than You Think

Picture this scene: a gulf-facing beach in Southwest Florida. It is prime time for snook. A fly casters steps off the beach and descends from the edge of the shoreline and into a trough. While wading along and casting he waits for the first snook to bite. Readying for another cast he was startled by a voice from behind: "Nice cast there, young fella. Too bad all the snook are behind you."

That angler was me and I was not only surprised by the gentleman's voice but his advice. He motioned for me to join him up on the sand. I did so, and for the better part of a half hour we both watched as snook after snook moved along the shoreline, at times traveling up from the trough to seek a meal in literally inches of water. After my new friend continued on his beach walk I returned to fishing, this time standing on terra firma. I salvaged the morning and caught a few snook. Needless to say I was amazed at the sight and thankful for the words of wisdom.

A nice surf-caught snook on the fly.   (Photo credit: Marcia Foosaner)

While that event happened many years ago, it was one I never forgot. From that point forward, whenever I approach the edge of a shoreline I make it a point to fan cast the area before entering the water. After all, the shallow edge where water meets land is in essence a form of structure. I've carried through with that discipline under a wide ranging set of flyfishing situations, from striped bass feeding on sand eels in mere inches of water to migrating silver salmon on remote coastal Alaska streams, and all stops in between. Similar circumstances are often encountered when fishing sod banks, grass flats, sand bars, or any other form of structure that abuts shallow water. Fish, even big fish, frequent thin water close to shore or to shoreline structure. While early mornings, evenings, and the hours under the cover of darkness are prime times for fish to venture close to shore, certain times of the year will see fish roaming the shallow edge even during daylight hours.

Low Tide Reconnaissance

Regardless of where you fish along the East Coast, it pays to check out new places and to take exploratory jaunts during periods of low tide. Extreme moon tides are the best since they reveal the most. Much can be seen and learned when the tide is out. I once happened upon a small configuration of rocks in the back of a large harbor that consistently held fish during the flood. I never would have seen them had I not gone looking while the water was completely drained. One memorable

Low water is one of the best times to scout an area, especially during periods of spring and neap tides.   (Photo credit: Rich Santos)

excursion involved a boat but resulted in a new find for fly fishing the surf. Having launched at dead low during a full moon tide I decided to check out an area I had yet to fish that season. I motored along at literally idle speed over a section of water that I'd fished for almost thirty years. I thought I knew that area like the back of my hand, until I felt and heard the slight scraping. Upon circling back over the spot I saw the tips of what looked like a cluster of man-made structures beneath the surface. These "rocks" were never visible during any phase of tide or season before, but with the extreme low my engine skeg just kissed the tops. I made note of the structure by hitting the MOB button on my GPS and then later that day fished the location from the beach. I came to learn that in the 1950s jetty stones destined for one of the local harbors were inadvertently dropped in that location. While the location doesn't always produce fish there are times of the year when it comes alive. A scuffed skeg was a small price to pay for that kind of treasure find. For the fly angler fishing the surf, it is the in-close structure that most affects the feeding habits and daily migratory movements of gamefish. Unlike traditional surf casters whose equipment allows for distances to be achieved out to second and third level breakers, the fly angler is limited by approximately 100 feet of fly line. Therefore, acute attention must be paid to any and all forms of structure, no matter how subtle, that exist literally at one's feet and extend to within the near shore beach zone.

Chapter Five

Strategies, Tactics, and Essential Gear

W hen looking out upon a vast body of water for the first time, whether an ocean, an expansive flat, a back bay, a large sound, or a coastal harbor, an angler might sense a bit of trepidation or at least some uncertainty about where to cast a fly. Even seasoned anglers will feel challenged by new and different water. I recall once motoring through a maze of channels and cuts that lead to Florida Bay. To me, most of the terrain and water that we passed by seemed like good places to stop and fish. But my guide continually shook his head in the negative and kept focused on a distant objective. Had I been fishing alone I might never have reached the ultimate honey hole destination, for I would have stopped at every likely looking piece of water to prospect the area. Obviously my guide's wisdom came from years of experience on the water and an intimate knowledge of the whereabouts of the tarpon we were after.

While that event took place on a flats skiff, the same scenarios play out in the surf or other wadable waters. Consistently successful fly anglers plan each outing and where they will fish rather than leave the day's results to happenstance. Any outdoor activity is always subject to change due to nature's variables, and while many anglers can only go fishing when the opportunities arise, having a sound angling strategy that encompasses the span of time one is on the water is always helpful. I may not always know where the day will take me and where I might end up on beach, but I regularly plan where my fishing will begin. There are many factors that go into preparing a fishing plan and most of those elements come with experience and acquired knowledge. However, there are some fundamentals that can get you on track to dependable surf fly angling and help make the most of your fishing time. Building personal fishing strategies around these schemes will give the fly angler a decided advantage, and enable contingency plans in the event the primary strategy doesn't pan out.

Time of Day

Regardless of where you fish along the East Coast, there are three universally accepted prime times for fly fishing the surf: predawn into the early morning hours; the time period immediately before and after dusk; and during the dark hours of the night. Fishing at these times will often offer some of the best fishing windows.

Early morning will find fish cruising the shallow edges of the surf zone, often no more than several feet from shore. These are often residual fish that remain from the previous night's feeding forays or fish that have keyed in on baitfish that linger in shallow water throughout near shore surf areas.

One example of this approach is best exemplified by Northeast striped bass that feed on masses of sand eels. When sand eels are present in an area, they will move in to the shallows at dusk to burrow in the sand. Bass become conditioned to this behavior and move in concert with the small eels to feed. Those same eels will then emerge from the sand, usually on an early morning flood time. Bass are conditioned to that behavior as well and will feed accordingly. Other gamefish along the East Coast also follow similar patterns of prey movements. An angler who keys in on those behaviors and the false dawn to post-dawn hours will have a decided advantage in maximizing time on the water.

Pre-dawn and the time period around sunrise will produce results north and south along the East Coast.

Bass and snook alike respond well to a setting sun.

The time period of one half hour before dusk to one half hour after sun set has a well earned reputation as being the "magic hour" for surf anglers. For those with limited time to fly fish the surf, this is often an ideal window of opportunity. Late spring and summer months allow an angler to reach the water after work and still enjoy plenty of productive fishing time. Many successful conventional surf anglers and fly anglers will fish this time period exclusively. This is a strategy that will pay off well in the long run. I've enjoyed some very reliable results over the years fishing this dusk scenario. Fish will often move very near shore at these times, providing ideal opportunities for fly anglers.

Once the sun sets a transition begins—an angler can typically expect to catch fish as darkness approaches—but immediately thereafter a fish's visual sensory system undergoes a mode change. The cones and rods of a fish's retina adjust to the changing light conditions, enabling it to better see under the cover of darkness. This transformation will often result in a lull in activity for a short period before inshore activity resumes. In my experience—and if fish are around—a bite will continue for about an hour and half after sunset. From that point on most surf anglers will generally see renewed activity during the late hours of the night from about 11 p.m. to 3 a.m. Obviously, that is a general rule of thumb contingent upon other variables such as tide phase, current, moon phase, wind, and weather. Fish don't always follow the

Late day redfish.   (Photo credit: Nick Angelo)

Skinny-water afternoon snook.

established rules of engagement. I've enjoyed many evening sessions of fly fishing for striped bass from the surf that began at dusk and lasted for more than three hours, with consistent action, after which the bite shut down until the following morning. Very often, the spring and fall months will see excellent fishing even during the daytime hours. In the spring, it becomes more a matter of conducive water temperature, while in the fall, fish often have the feedbag on as they move through their migratory travels.

Fishing the surf at night is also productive when daytime temperatures in summer months reach high levels and move beyond the comfort zone of inshore gamefish species. Both bait and fish will remain offshore until cooler evening and night temperatures are more suitable to their physiology. Water temperature is but one variable in the fish-catching equation, yet at times it can be a critical one. Baitfish will also move inshore at night since darkness provides some measure of added protection from predators. At minimum, birds are no longer a threat and the visual acuity of gamefish is no longer at peak levels; different sensory mechanisms kick in to compensate for diminished sight. As long as baitfish remain close to shore, gamefish will too. Once darkness sets in, I will usually switch to darker flies in black and purple with traces of red. At night, profile and contrast are more important considerations than hue and tone.

Seasons

No matter where one fishes along the East Coast shoreline, spring and fall months are prime periods for the surf fly angler. Most gamefish will exhibit heightened activity at these times, whether the result of pre- or post-spawning activity or due to the abundance of baitfish and ideal water conditions. Concentrating one's surf fishing around these seasons places the angler on the water when opportunities are most prevalent. The hotter summer months can either be boom or bust depending on where the fishing occurs. In contrast, some Southeast inshore fishing might slow down during the heat of the day, but Northeast waters might enjoy a bonanza of migratory pelagic species like bonito or little tunny.

The fall is another time when great concentrations of fish move in mass migration mode from north to south. This activity is most prominent along the Northeast and mid-Atlantic segments of the coastline. For more southerly areas, the fall brings cooling water that stimulates indigenous fish to feed aggressively and during more times of day. It is quite possible that during peak fall fishing, surf anglers will experience the most intensely concentrated fishing of the year. For many, this season presents an opportunity for some of the best fishing both in terms of quantity and quality of fish. I know many Northeast anglers who save their vacation days for the

Seeing a pod of blitzing fall bass within casting distance from shore will get any fly angler's adrenaline pumping.

fall run. Simply put, a few weeks of this fast and furious fishing can in many ways make for a great year!

Once December rolls around, avid Northeast fly anglers will set sight on more southerly locales to keep the season alive. The most consistent wading activity throughout the colder months occurs in Florida. While most of the state will remain productive throughout the winter season, the Keys are by far the most consistent, along with other coastal states that border the Gulf of Mexico shoreline.

Moon Phases

Much has been written about the best moon phases for fishing the surf. In the final analysis, new moon and full moon phases both have their advocates. Some anglers will fish religiously for two or three days on either side of a new moon while others will totally ignore the new moon and concentrate all their efforts around the big tides of a full moon. I've fished both lunar phases, and while I give a slight edge to the new moon (based solely on my personal experiences), I am aware of many other surf anglers who do well under the influence of a full moon. In talking with a number of anglers, the most significant reason for either preference relates to the illumination of a full moon versus the dark side of a new moon. Fish are imprinted from fry stages to be wary of attack from predators in shallow water. During a full moon shadows can be cast upon the water that can trigger a flight response in gamefish and baitfish; shadows are associated with potential danger. In contrast, when the moon is positioned between the earth and the sun, the resulting dark side of the moon faces earth. Without reflective light from the sun those troublesome shadows are virtually nonexistent. That becomes a decided advantage with wary or skittish fish. Although tides are covered in the next segment, suffice to say that the linear alignment of earth, moon, and sun during both full and new moon phases create extra strong tides. For some species, that can be a beneficial byproduct as these deeper flood tides can play host to larger concentrations of baitfish. The challenge for the surf angler is to find locations under those conditions where a fly can still be properly presented to fish. The downside of moon tides is that if the high tide, for example, is very extreme, the angler might be placed out of position to effectively cast to fish-holding areas. I have been in situations during full moon phases where I was backed up so far in a marsh that I could not reach areas with a fly where fish were feeding. This highlights another issue when fishing high moon tides at night: be aware of your surroundings to avoid being stranded or encountering water heights that might pose a risk to your safety.

Tides and Currents

One of the most important factors for successful flyfishing in the surf is an understanding of tides and currents and their interrelationship. Having a working knowledge of why and how coastal water moves and how those flows affect baitfish and gamefish is critical to the surf fly angler. The positioning of the earth, moon, and sun in relation to each other, combined with their gravitational influences, work to create worldwide tidal movements. Tides are fundamentally generated by periodic bulging of earth's water both toward and away from the moon. This hydrodynamic phenomenon pushes inward to create high tides while water pulled in the opposite direction causes outward movement and, thus, low tides. As a result of the earth's rotation, two such cycles of bulging typically occur each day and cause tidal movements. Some locations may only experience one such tide cycle. The direct linear alignment of the earth, moon, and sun during new and full moon phases creates the strongest tides and currents. These cycles are known as "spring tides." At the other end of the spectrum are the much weaker "neap tides" that occur when the gravitational forces of the moon and sun are minimized by their perpendicular orientation to the earth. These tides arise during quarter-moon cycles.

Flood tide occurs as water levels rise throughout the inter-tidal zone and to a point where they reach maximum height and coastal penetration. The magnitude of that "reach" is influenced by specific coast line topography. The opposing ebb tide takes form as water levels recede and fall to the lowest point, known as low tide. Tides also produce currents. While tidal bulges move water vertically, currents move laterally or horizontally. Tidal currents are influenced by many factors, including:

Incoming water will cause fish to move deeper into cover.

intensity of tides; wind direction and strength; contour of the coast line; surface and subsurface structure like jetties, rock formations, and underwater boulders; channels; troughs; and areas where water funnels and accelerates. Water temperature can also affect current flows.

The distinction between tides and currents is significant since both flows influence movements and feeding behaviors of bait and gamefish. Fish will move deeper into intertidal areas on the flood and follow bait with retreating water. Fish like striped bass, redfish, bonefish, and permit will move on and off flats with flooding and ebbing tides. Fish will also feed deeper into marshes, grass lines, mangroves, harbors, and backcountry areas on high water, and again move out with falling water. Gamefish naturally gravitate toward areas of current where vulnerable prey can be ambushed. It takes a bit of learning and time on the water to appreciate how tides and currents affect fishing in your specific areas.

It took several years for me to fully understand one of my favorite fishing areas and to learn that there was a forty-five minute window of opportunity around a tide phase when the fish were most active along that particular stretch of beach. Interestingly enough, when I would move several hundred yards off that spot, a different set of tide and current variables required an alternative fishing strategy. The greater your inventory of fishing locations, the greater your ability to connect the dots and learn the best times to cast flies. One of the best pieces of advice I've ever received is that as long as you are able to find current and moving water, keep fishing. That guidance was highlighted a few seasons back when a friend caught the largest bass of his angling career just before slack water in an area that still had a slight current flow.

Wind

Wind is often viewed as the number one nemesis of saltwater fly anglers. While extreme winds certainly present challenging and often overwhelming casting conditions, moderate wind can be a surf angler's ally. Too many anglers put down the fly rods when the winds kick up. Smart fly anglers learn to cast into wind. One reason to do so is compelling: sustained periods of winds moving onto shore can move baitfish and gamefish closer to the surf zone and within casting distance of fly anglers who have the ability to overcome wind. At times, baitfish and gamefish will be in the whitewater foam immediately off the beach. An angler who gains proficiency casting a workable length of fly line will be in a better position to score results than someone who packs up the fly rod at the first sign of a breeze. I prefer using sink-tip lines when the wind kicks up so that the presentation of the fly will allow it to sink beneath the waves that accompany higher winds. A low sidearm cast works well to minimize the effects of oncoming wind resistance. Be cognizant of wind direction and the fly's flight, since a wind that moves across an angler's body from the casting

If head-on winds along the beach get too challenging, try finding a protected lee where you might locate a few fish.

arm to stripping arm can drive a fly into the angler. I've had weighted flies hit my fishing hat with enough speed to emulate the sound of a .22-caliber short round, and a few have stuck. Be careful. There are also times when wind can actually aid in the cast. Throwing an open loop with the wind at your back will help your fly line sail farther than you may have thought possible.

Prevailing and seasonal winds are a given and consistent reality of coastal fly fishing and should be factored into any outing's game plan. If winds are indeed too strong for effective fly fishing, an angler can often salvage the day by seeking a lee-side location where wind is blocked or wind intensity is diminished.

Tactical Wading

Some surf anglers prefer to stay put in one known productive spot while others are constantly on the move. I am a member of the latter group, opting to seek fish out rather than wait for them to come to me. That approach is not one of aimlessly walking about but rather part of a strategy that embraces many of the elements previously discussed: season and time of day; tide phase; current flow; and bait movements. How, where, and when one fishes is determined through assimilation of that knowledge and projecting where the bite is most likely to occur. I typically know where I want to be at specific points throughout the day or the tide. This becomes a personal journey for each and every surf fly angler since experience is the best teacher.

I've watched fly anglers remain in one spot for an entire tide cycle only to later lament that the fish just weren't there. There comes a point of diminishing return where it is time for a change of scenery. After all, what is there to lose? If you are not catching, move on. Sometimes just a short change of venue might lead you to discover a new piece of structure that fish migrate toward during a particular phase of the tide. Some anglers are hesitant to make a move for fear of losing out if fish do eventually show. As previously stated, fly fishing the surf is a journey of discovery. But it is much more fulfilling when you discover the fish rather than let them find you.

While surf fishing in general terms, regardless of the methods employed, is a fairly social sport, many of the legends of the game are somewhat solitary practitioners—and with good reason. Countless hours on the water and time spent exploring new and different areas should come with a benefit; and that benefit is the rewards that the effort yields. Put in more surf time than the next angler and you deserve your own sanctuaries and honey holes. Be willing to venture off the beaten path and beyond the point where everyone else's boot tracks end. Some of my most remarkable fishing and outdoor sights have come with just hoofing it farther than others. In my book, finding fish or following their movements is always much more productive over time than adopting the wait-and-see approach.

Be Prepared

There is nothing more frustrating than being on a beach or on some expansive sand flat, only to realize that you left a critical piece of angling gear back in your vehicle. We have all been there. On one such occasion I had taken a long summer beach walk to wet wade a location where I was fortunate to catch some double-digit size bluefish on flies. I had just landed one such twelve-pound fish, and reached for a pair of pliers that weren't there. I had left them on my wading belt in the back of my truck, that was now two miles from where I held an agitated chopper. Extracting a deeply taken fly from the toothy maw of a large bluefish without a tool can be a potentially dangerous proposition. I never again forgot my pliers. The same can be said for other essential pieces of equipment. What I carry with me depends on the time of year and the species I pursue, but some items are just more indispensable than others. Here are some that might make your day wading more comfortable and enjoyable.

If you are fishing the Northeast surf during the spring or late fall months, or a southerly locale in winter, a pair of good waders is the first essential. A pair of breathable waders will serve you well throughout all the East Coast. If you fish in colder parts of the region and need more protection, just wear fleece pants under

A collection of essential items should be assembled to make the fly angler's time during wade fishing as comfortable as possible.

the waders. You can use either boot-foot or stocking-foot waders. I prefer the latter, since I can then match them to a more comfortable and precisely fitting wading boot, which these days are constructed much like high-quality hiking boots. For those surf anglers who like to walk extended distances during a day's outing, this is the way to go. A gravel guard over each boot will help prevent sand and small pebbles from getting into the boot and causing discomfort or damage to the boot foot. Carry an extra pair of boot laces. It's no fun trying to craft makeshift laces from leader material. For safety's sake wear a wading belt. In the event of unexpected dunking the belt will help hold off water from filling the waders too rapidly. A wading staff can also be helpful for those who might venture to places with uncertain footing. A set of pull-on or strap-on spikes can be carried for those situations where slick rocks or jetties are encountered. In warmer months, I will wet wade in shorts or long fishing pants with either a pair of wading boots or flats booties.

A pack of some sort is also another piece of useful equipment. The pack can come in the form of a small back pack, fanny pack, chest pack, or a set of differently sized pouches. I like to combine things and prefer a fanny pack or side chest pack with several attached pouches for carrying a variety of other incidental items. When

Metal cleat boots or slip-on cleats are essential when fishing from jetties or slippery boulders and rocks.

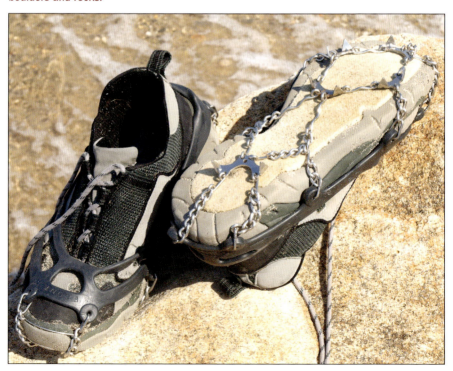

Pouches, in addition to small packs, offer lightweight storage capacity when on a wade-fishing outing.

I plan an entire day on the beach (two tide cycles) I will carry a small backpack that I can use to hold lunch and water and a light rain jacket.

The pack and pouches I carry are used to hold items like fly wallets, leader materials, clippers, pliers, a pocket knife, bug repellent, sun screen, glasses, a night light, a small waterproof digital camera, spare reel or spool, a small pair of binoculars, and a Boga-Grip. And don't forget a stripping basket and a pair of good polarized sunglasses.

'Yak and Wade

Many saltwater fly anglers are now employing personal watercraft to enhance and maximize their surf- and wade-fishing experiences. Kayaks have become the platform of choice for fly anglers. Like many anglers, I use my kayak as a conveyance to get me to places I can wade, that are beyond reach of hiking or inaccessible in any way but from the water. While many of these same places can be accessed with shallow draft boats and trolling motors or push poles, kayaks are a much more practical and cost-effective alternative if the distances to be traveled aren't too extreme. You can tote along additional equipment for a full-day outing to fishing areas out of bounds to many other anglers. A kayak can efficiently and economically expand the range and scope of a wading angler's world.

A kayak can help you find areas of wading seclusion.   (Photo credit: Rich Santos)

Kayaks can be either of the sit-in or sit-on-top variety and rigged from the simple to the sublime with all sorts of gadgets and electronics. But for purposes of getting an angler to and from wading spots, simplicity works best. Devices for securing rods, paddles, and gear are essentials for the minimalist. Anything beyond that best serves the angler who actually fishes from the 'yak. The most important piece of kayaking gear is a personal floatation device that should be worn whenever the kayak is underway. You just never know when it will be needed in a life-threatening situation. My canoe once flipped in fast water while on a smallmouth bass float trip down the Delaware River. Were it not for an inflatable life vest I would not be here writing these words. It doesn't always happen to the other guy! If you are fishing cold water that requires waders, it is prudent to remove the waders as you move from one spot to the next. Spills from kayaks are common occurrences and having waders on in those situations can be extremely dangerous, especially in early spring when hypothermia can result from immersion in cold water.

Beach Fishing Safety

Bad things can happen quickly around water, so caution should always be exercised when engaged in surf fly fishing or any wade-fishing activities. Each new season along the East Coast brings sad news of some angler being swept from a jetty or sand bar or falling from rocks. Lives have been lost, and I speak from personal experience when I say that no matter how experienced or careful one might be, surprises can and will occur. I have fly fished one stretch of Long Island beach for more than thirty years and pride myself on knowing that piece of surf like the back of my hand. I've explored every nook and cranny for miles. A few years back while fishing a late spring tide, I learned the hard way how a nasty nor'easter the previous winter changed the profile and contours of a portion of this familiar beach.

My wanderings took me to a long sand bar that jutted our toward deeper water. I had fished this bar many times in the past and whenever I am on this section of beach. It is a location I know very well. By the time dusk arrived the striped bass were active on the incoming tide, and it was one of those evenings when it appeared as if the bass hit the fly on every cast. I moved laterally along this bar, catching bass the entire way. Upon reaching the terminal point of the sand bar that protruded to deeper water, the bass turned on even more than they had been, gorging nonstop on sand eels. The fast pace of this fly fishing kept me engaged until well after sunset. When I finally had enough, I walked to a location where I knew the bar connected to a shallow sand bridge that lead back to the beach. I stepped off the bar and immediately found myself in water over the top of my waders. The winter storms had created a deep trough where the shallow sand bridge had been. Fortunately, a tightly secured wading belt stemmed the flow of water into the waders long enough for me to move back onto the bar. Slightly rattled, but intact, I slowly moved about the bar, and aided by my flashlight I located a safe crossing point back to the beach. An incident that could have had dire consequences gave me a good laugh on the walk back to my truck. But the experience was a lesson learned and retained.

Here are a few safety pointers that can help keep you safe, comfortable, and fly fishing for a long time to come.

1. Rather than plodding ahead while wading, take it slow. Shuffle your feet laterally as you move instead of taking big blind steps. This will help prevent you from falling into a pothole, tripping over an unexpected rock, or stepping on something that could cause harm, like the stinger of a ray. Plus, you'll spook less fish.
2. If you are unsure of your footing, use a wading staff to help with balance. When standing on slick rocks or jetties wear a pair of studded soles or slip-on cleats.
3. Never wade beyond your own physical limits. While there are some extreme fly anglers who swim in wet suits to distant rocks upon which they perch, that game is not for everyone. Avoid wading into areas of strong currents, and become familiar with the area you intend to fish. It is sometime easier getting to a spot than it is getting back to dry land safely.

Casting

1. To optimize the casting stroke, rod, reel, and line should be matched and balanced. While this may seem an obvious suggestion I am often surprised to see some of the tackle anglers attempt to use for fly fishing. Very often anglers will mistakenly overweight a rod by one, two, or even three line weights, expecting that this will compensate for less than ideal casting technique. The erroneous belief is that the extra line weight will better load a rod and facilitate a longer cast. Precision in design is a hallmark of contemporary fly rods and fly lines and, therefore, the line used should match the rod's weight designation. Reel size should also be matched to feel balanced in the rod hand of the caster. There are some benefits of over-lining by one line weight, especially when short, quick casts are required, but mastering the fundamentals of sound casting techniques using balanced tackle should be the goal of every serious surf fly angler.

2. When beginning to learn the art of fly casting, several key components of the cast should be practiced to maximize accuracy and distance. Be cognizant of the

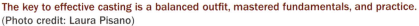

The key to effective casting is a balanced outfit, mastered fundamentals, and practice. (Photo credit: Laura Pisano)

line's complete flight and how the line behaves on both the back cast and the forward cast. Slow down the casting stoke and allow the line to straighten or unfurl on the back cast. Pay attention to timing. One indication of a good back cast and that the line that has completely straightened is a slight tug you feel at the terminal point of the back cast. This distinctive pull is the signal to begin the forward casting stroke. With practice, a caster will learn to feel that precise moment when the forward cast should begin. It is somewhat of an epiphany, a moment when it all comes together. A tug on the back cast and line shooting efficiently through the guides of a fly rod on the forward cast are signals the pieces of the cast are fully understood. Once you make that ideal cast, you will not forget the feel of it and that will become your template for all other casts. The optimum cast will allow line to load the rod and prepare the line for the forward power stroke. Don't overpower the forward cast. Use enough power to effortlessly move the line through the forward cast to unload the rod's energy.

3. Learn to shoot line on the back cast as well as on the forward cast. This simple technique involves allowing short lengths of line to move through the fingers, as line is pulled through the guides and extends the back cast. That motion increases the line's momentum and works to generate a greater load on the rod. In turn, that adds more power to the forward cast.

4. Many anglers who become involved in saltwater fly fishing most often have roots in freshwater fishing for trout and bass. Each form of fly fishing has its own challenges and I wouldn't want to minimize either, but the biggest challenge that converts from freshwater to saltwater fly fishing typically encounter is with slowing down the casting stroke. Small-stream trout anglers are used to the more rapid and frequent false casting strokes associated with "drying" flies during false casts, since they often have less line in the air. In salt water, false casting ideally is kept to a minimum. You want to load the rod quickly with one or two false casts and then shoot line to the target area. Situations where this is valuable are when sight casting to feeding and cruising; fish like tarpon, bonefish, stripers, redfish, and quick up-and-down mini-blitzes of fast fish like little tunny, bonito, jacks, or Spanish mackerel. This also applies to fish cruising the edge of the surf line. It is also impractical and inefficient to keep long lengths of heavy high-density lines in the air for too long. It is counterproductive.

5. Although in many small-stream situations a fly angler can keep a measured amount of line in the air throughout numerous false casts, it is imperative in salt water to learn to employ the double haul to increase line speed and maximize distance. The two major benefits of the double haul are that the technique allows the caster to make more powerful casts with a relatively small amount of effort, and allows for the formation of tighter line loops. I have found that freshwater converts who've

and forefinger. Rotating the wrist and gathering line with the lower three fingers moves the fly along in small increments.

DOUBLE OVERHAND RETRIEVE

This retrieve is ideal for moving a fly rapidly through the water. It is very effective for fast moving pelagic species of fish like Atlantic bonito, little tunny, and Spanish mackerel. Other gamefish will also respond to the retrieve when feeding on fast-moving bait. With this technique the angler places the rod under the armpit and uses two hands to retrieve the fly. Line is gathered with a motion that moves the hands one over the other to move the fly through the water. This method requires a different hook set that has the angler strip set by pulling on the line while simultaneously lifting the rod vigorously.

COMBINATION RETRIEVES

Fish will respond differently to specific retrieves. It often takes some experimentation to determine the retrieve that will stimulate fish to strike a fly. Preferences can vary from day-to-day. One of the best ways to test the reaction of fish is by mixing up retrieves and combining techniques. For example, if a simple long pull retrieve isn't working, try a long and short pull in combination with a fast and slow retrieve or a wrist flick.

MENDING LINE

One line management technique that is of value to the surf fly angler is known as mending. This method works best in moving water where the fly is best fished in a naturally drifting fashion, floating unimpeded with the movement of current. While mending was first used when fly fishing for steelhead, salmon, and trout in rivers, it holds an important place in the surf angler's retrieve arsenal. What this technique entails is casting the fly up-current and, as it flows through the course of the drift, picking line up off the water and moving that line back upstream. This accomplishes three things: it allows the fly to drift naturally with the current; the fly is not at all restrained by line tension; and the fly can remain in the strike zone longer. Fish may see this as a bait form just moving with the flow of water. The inherent action of the fly drifting in this manner will motivate fish to strike, as will the terminal point of the drift where the line eventually tightens and the fly moves up the water column.

Stripping Basket

One of the most important pieces of equipment a surf fly angler can use is a stripping basket that is worn about the caster's waist. If line is allowed to fall into the surf or into current as it is retrieved, it can tangle or move with the current, prevent-

A stripping basket is required for controlling and managing fly line in the surf and in areas with a sweeping current.

ing an efficient next cast. The basket is used to manage line in loose coils during the retrieve so that it sits tangle free and ready for the follow-up cast. Once the cast is made and the retrieve is started, the angler pulls line through the guides and places it in the basket.

Quality stripping baskets have numerous molded cones affixed to the bottom of the basket so the coils of line stay somewhat neat and untangled. When the subsequent cast is made and line propels forward, line shoots easily from the basket and through the guides.

Line Contact

Whether engaged in the act of casting or retrieving, it is essential to maintain constant contact with the line. Only by doing such can an angler stay in touch with the fly. Failure to do so will result in missed hook sets and missed fish. Contact with line extends from the cast, to the retrieve, to the hook set. One technique I like to employ when casting to specific targets like visibly feeding fish is to keep the fingers of the retrieve hand loosely formed around the line, almost functioning like an additional guide. In this way the line will move freely through the fingers. When the fly reaches the target area the fingers can close quickly around the line and be ready to get the fly in motion without ever losing contact with the line.

Good fly fishing is where you find it. (Photo credit: Nick Angelo)

No matter the size, all gamefish take on a fly rod with worthy catches.
(Photo credit: Nick Angelo)

Chapter Seven

East Coast Saltwater Gamefish

The East Coast of the United States in its entirety, from Maine to Florida, plays host to abundant and fertile fisheries tailor-made for fly fishing the surf. Both indigenous and migrating species provide active and consistent sport for fly anglers throughout most of the year. It is quite possible for the willing Northeast angler to be occupied with flyfishing opportunities from April through December. Moving down the seaboard to the mid-Atlantic and Southeast regions, seasons extend farther into the year, to the point where, depending upon weather conditions, Florida anglers can enjoy year-round flyfishing opportunities.

While fly fishing from the beach and wade fishing have been popular in the Southeast for many decades, it was unquestionably the resurgence of striped bass that fueled interest in saltwater surf fly fishing throughout the Northeast and mid-Atlantic regions. Striped bass stocks experienced unprecedented recovery from the waters of North Carolina and the Chesapeake up along the Maine coastline. The entire East Coast was a beneficiary of this revitalized surf fishery. New fly fishermen entered the sport in unprecedented numbers, while many old salts proclaimed the renaissance to be the way it once was. Many freshwater anglers converted to the new saltwater arena. Most were trout and bass anglers accustomed to wade fishing after their quarry. Those anglers were thrilled, since they could now consistently catch somewhat bigger fish on the flies, fish that would pull harder than the hatchery trout many were used to catching.

Adding to the Northeast bounty of striped bass were the equally revitalized stocks of bluefish, a return of weakfish, and the consistent appearance of pelagic species into nearshore waters. Fish such as false albacore, Atlantic bonito, and Spanish mackerel energized the interest and imagination of any fly angler choosing to pursue these gamefish from the surf. Fly anglers fishing the more southerly shallows of the East Coast enjoyed strong stocks of resident fish like spotted seatrout, bonefish, and permit and the positive effects of enlightened fisheries management for snook and redfish, two of the more popular gamefish pursued by wading anglers in the surf. Equally as abundant have been the diverse gamefish species of the mid-Atlantic states that merge into a melting pot with both northern species moving south and southern species traveling north, all meeting in the middle.

Anglers now travel from all over the world to sample the East Coast's wealth of sport fish. Thousands of miles of shoreline, harbors, inlets, bays, flats, mangrove islands, and enriched backwaters play host to fertile and abundant fisheries. Cast a fly anywhere in those waters and you just might fool some superb gamefish to eat.

The primary East Coast surf species available to the wading angler through-out the range of the Atlantic seaboard include striped bass, bluefish, weakfish, fluke, hickory shad, American shad, Atlantic bonito, little tunny, spotted seatrout, Spanish mackerel, croakers, black drum, redfish, snook, bonefish, jacks, permit, pompano, and even tarpon.

The following profiles are of the most common saltwater species that the fly angler will encounter when fly fishing along the more than 2,000 miles of Atlantic coastline of the United States, and more than 28,000 miles of nooks, crannies, and appendages that comprise the even more expansive tidal shoreline. Each profile also includes some techniques and tips for catching these species with a fly rod.

Striped Bass (*Morone saxatilis*)

Northeast and mid-Atlantic fly anglers have had a passionate affair with striped bass longer than with any other species of fish. The reason for this dedication is the striper's extended availability along the striper coast from about April of each year until late winter, with bass of mixed sizes willing to eat flies during the entire season. The striped bass is a fish for the masses, since it is readily catchable and within

Striped bass.

easy reach of surf and wading fly anglers. You need not own a boat to enjoy world-class striper fishing. Bass frequent the surf close to beaches, bays, harbors, inlets, grassy estuaries, sand and gravel flats, tidal creeks, eddies, pools, and rivers. Bass also come in a variety of sizes, from small school fish to specimens well over fifty, sixty, and seventy pounds. While bass most eager to strike flies in the surf will be stout school-sized fish in the five- to twelve-pound range, a significant number of big fish, thirty pounds or more, fall to flies each season. Some of the largest specimens of bass caught on the fly are taken when they feed on large baits like adult Atlantic menhaden (bunker), shad, or herring.

Stripers are built heavy and solid, with broad, powerful tails and trademark stripes along both sides of the body. Bass are built for quick bursts of speed as they pursue prey. They are strong, dogged fighters. At the time of this writing, the largest IGFA striped bass caught on a fly weighed in at an impressive sixty-four pounds, eight ounces. Larger bass of more than 100 pounds have been found in the nets of commercial fishermen. Stripers in excess of forty or fifty pounds in size will strike flies. Though that is more the exception than the rule, the possibility certainly exists for fly anglers fishing the waters of the Northeast and mid-Atlantic coasts to catch bass in excess of twenty or thirty pounds.

Most bass that travel the striper coast—and that are accessible to surf anglers—are primarily from either the Chesapeake Bay or Hudson River stocks. Stripers are anadromous, meaning they live predominantly in salt water but spend time in fresh water as well. After leaving their wintering grounds in Maryland and Virginia, stripers return from the salt to their natal freshwater rivers to spawn. Once the procreation urge is satisfied, bass move out from fresh water, and begin a transition back to salt water. Bass will infiltrate inland waters and move up the mid-Atlantic and Northeast coast. Starting about mid-April, bass can be caught in New Jersey, off the New York Bight, and along the western areas of Long Island. As the season progresses, bass gradually flood into all areas around Long Island and up the coast to all of New England.

The spring migration represents a unique opportunity for fly anglers fishing the surf. At that time of year, bass travel close to shore and will become active in shallow backwater areas and harbors, locations that offer the wading angler numerous opportunities. On the flipside of the spring migration, the fall run also sees bass move very close to shore. During both seasons, it is likely for a fly angler to catch bass in the surf wash literally feet and often inches from shore.

Striped bass are essentially inshore fish and, as such, provide numerous fly-angling opportunities for nearshore wading and boat anglers. Stripers show a marked preference for boulders and rocks, as one of its nicknames—rockfish—implies, as well as jetties, pilings, docks, piers, riprap, and other forms of visible or submerged structure. They can also be caught in open deep water and on sand and gravel flats, in literally inches of water. Sizable sand and gravel flats exist throughout the striper's range, with a growing number of fly fishermen pursuing bass in those situations. Wading these flats is a sight-fishing phenomenon comparable in many respects to bonefishing and casting to tailing redfish; it is one of the most challenging ways to take striped bass on a fly rod.

Fly fishing along the striper coast is a diverse game. There are many enjoyable ways to catch this superior gamefish on the fly rod. Stripers are very egalitarian—they frequent a variety of habitats and are accessible to all styles of fishing. They are especially receptive to flies fished in the surf, and are available to anglers who fish the wee hours of the morning or those who fish the vampire shift under the cover of darkness. Bass can also be caught quite regularly throughout the day, with tides, season, and bait availability being the key drivers.

While stripers are typically the first Northeast fish of the season to tug at a fly line, they are also notably the last, especially the larger specimens, which then move down the coast to the mid-Atlantic to stage for the winter months.

Bluefish (*Pomatomus saltatrix*)

Bluefish are caught throughout the total range of the East Coast. They are insatiable feeders, known to regurgitate their last meal so they can keep on feeding. Bluefish are ideal fish for the fly angler since they are often easy to catch, and often

Bluefish.   (Photo credit: Ken Ekelund)

frequent areas close to the shoreline. While blues can at times get selective, they are generally indiscriminate eaters and have no reservations about consuming their own young or anything else that can fit into their mouths. If some unfortunate prey is too big to be ingested whole, a bluefish simply uses it razor-sharp teeth and viselike jaws to ferociously chop it down to size. Some of the biggest specimens of bluefish are caught on flies when young-of-the-year bluefish—called snappers—are present in large numbers during the late summer. Big popping bugs and large flies work well at that time of year. Casting hookless plugs and then playing the bait-and-switch game with flies is also an exciting way to catch big bluefish that frequent close-to-shore structure.

As opportunistic predators, bluefish actively feed on a wide variety of bait. During the chaos of the fall run, large frenzied bluefish even attempt to eat school-sized striped bass and keeper-sized blackfish. They do so in vicious fashion, usually biting off the tails of large prey so they become incapacitated and can't swim. I've had my fly returned to me on many occasions in the mouth of a small bass that had no body. The largest of the bluefish species are referred to as "choppers" or alligators, monikers that pointedly define aggressive behavioral traits and characteristics.

Bluefish frequently roam very close to beaches during the spring and fall, searching out massive schools of sand eels, menhaden, silversides, finger mullet, butterfish, squid, and various other whitebait. When they find and key in on those baits, the ensuing scene is nothing short of complete carnage. Bluefish engaged in this wild feeding frenzy often cause harried prey to flee from the water and jump onto land to avoid capture, in essence committing mass suicide as an alternative to being eaten.

Bluefish are long, physically muscular fish with powerful forked tails. Their ominous trademark is a mouth full of razor-sharp, serrated teeth that can easily shred prey. Bluefish are very aggressive and strike at most anything that crosses their paths, including flies. Rarely is there a need to use intricately tied patterns with these fish—elaborate or simple, flies are all the same to blues. Yet, there are times when bluefish exhibit a selectivity that can be frustrating. This occurs most often when they sip smaller rainbait such as small sand eels or bay anchovies, or cruise through swarms of small crabs or a clam worm swarm. During these times of selectivity, it is the fly fisherman who has the distinct advantage. Having encountered these lockjaw situations while surf fishing, I have found that flies far and away prove more effective than other forms of conventional or spin fishing lures.

Bluefish are an ocean-going species that regularly frequent inshore areas, and like striped bass, they have become a favorite target species of surf fly anglers. Their migration along the East Coast parallels much the same patterns as those of stripers. They work their way up the coast and then into all bays, harbors, and inlets. Blues are tailor-made for the fly rodder; they are fish that strike flies with reckless abandon and fight with aggressiveness and determination. Many surf fly anglers who hook into trophy bluefish are often fooled into thinking the fish at the end of their lines are much larger striped bass. Hook into a ten- or fifteen-pound bluefish on the fly rod—in the surf—and you will believe it to be a much bigger striped bass. The largest recorded fly-caught bluefish in IGFA records weighed in at nineteen pounds, twelve ounces.

Bluefish are one of the easiest fish species to catch on flies, eager to strike at most any fly one might cast to them. One of the most exciting ways to catch them—especially the larger specimens—is with big topwater popping flies. The visual experience of seeing a large bluefish attempt to terminate the existence of an oversized popper is quite the adrenaline rush. Often, multiple big fish will slash at the artificial simultaneously. The key to hooking up is not to strike back until you feel the weight of the fish. A common mistake of some fly anglers is to strip set on the visual splashes. This isn't a trout rise—wait until the bulk of the fish is felt, then set the hook and hang on.

Weakfish (*Cynoscion regalis*)

Also known by its Native American name, squeteague, weakfish are sometimes referred to as gray trout or summer trout. This highly coveted fish is the Northeast relative of the Southern spotted seatrout. Weakfish tend toward higher average weights than seatrout; the largest specimens are known as tiderunners. Their stocks, more than most other species of the Northeast, have succumbed to dramatic cyclical reductions; at one point the fish was on the brink of being endangered. But their numbers are now slowly on the rise, and savvy surf anglers are once again connecting with weakfish.

During the initial weeks of spring, weakfish move into back bays, harbors, inlets, and other areas with tidal flows. As with early season striped bass, most of the early activity takes place in the more westerly areas of their range, where water heats up first and bait becomes active.

Weakfish are long and lean, with a distinctly troutlike body shape. Their flanks and back display dark markings, and the fish are adorned with an overall appealing coloration that includes hues and tones of rose, lavender, olive green, copper, blue, and even traces of gold. Two of the most defining features of weakfish are their yellow anal and pelvic fins. The name, weakfish, originates from the frail mouth of the fish and does not at all imply that the fish itself lacks strength. Quite to the contrary, the weakfish is a worthy adversary on the fly rod.

Weakfish initially enter Northeast waters in April and May for the express purpose of spawning. Their habitat preferences include bays, estuaries, tidal creeks, and the surf or other areas with sandy bottoms. Once their spawning mission is

Weakfish.   (Photo credit: Alberto Knie)

satisfied, weakfish remain in those areas to feed and until their southerly migration begins in the fall. While their defined range is quite extensive—from Massachusetts to Florida—the vast majority of weakfish spend the summers from Delaware to the waters off Long Island.

Weakfish feed on a variety of food sources, including shrimp, crabs, crustaceans and mollusks, spearing, killies, small herring and butterfish, menhaden, and any number of other small baitfish. Weakfish feed throughout much of the water column and readily strike flies. Most weakfish caught on flies range between one and six pounds, but tiderunners can reach weights in excess of pounds. During past peak weakfish cycles in the Northeast, it was not uncommon to see catches of tiderunners of ten, twelve, or even fourteen pounds. The largest weakfish taken on a fly was a fish caught in Delaware Bay and pulled the scale down to fourteen pounds, two ounces.

Like their Southern seatrout cousins, Northern weakfish have a predilection for brightly colored flies. Patterns sporting colors of red, yellow, chartreuse, or any of the hot tones work well. Standard patterns matching local baitfish can be modified to highlight those hues.

Spotted Seatrout (*Cynoscion nebulosus*)

Spotted seatrout or speckled trout are one of the most prolific and sought-after species in the Southeast and in the Southern portion of the mid-Atlantic region. While the total range of the species occurs from New York to the Gulf of Mexico, the predominant availability of seatrout is from Virginia to the Texas Gulf Coast. Seatrout are an excellent fly-rod species readily available to wading anglers.

This smaller "cousin" of the Northern weakfish averages about two to three pounds, and nineteen to twenty-five inches in length. Seatrout have distinct circular black spots on the back and upper flank portions of their bodies and on the fins and

Spotted seatrout.   (Photo credit: Rich Santos)

tails. The body is void of scales and has a soft dorsal fin. Two canine teeth located in the front of the upper jaw are a signature characteristic of seatrout.

Trout feed on small crustaceans, shrimp, and a variety of baitfish. Shrimp are a preferred food source, so fly patterns of that genre are very effective. Specks show a marked inclination for shallow water, estuaries, grass beds, and back bays. The largest seatrout are usually female, called sows, and will consume large baits like menhaden, pinfish, and mullet. The heaviest spotted seatrout on record and caught on fly was a true "gator" of fifteen pounds, six ounces.

Speckled trout have a preference for shallow bays, flats, and estuaries that contain grass or oyster beds. The spring and summer months will find trout in shallow water areas, while the cooler fall water temperatures motivate specks to seek deep water. General migration patterns, from shallow water to deep, and the reverse, are governed primarily by water temperatures and spawning cycles. Trout are very receptive to striking artificial lures, and will do so throughout the seasons; flies are especially effective.

A general rule of thumb when wading after seatrout is to fish shallow water in the morning and evening and look for pockets of deeper water during the heat of the day. Areas worth prospecting when wade fishing are: close-to-shore troughs and drop-offs, potholes, and deep water around grass and oyster flats. Hot-colored flies tied with chartreuse, hot pink, cerise, yellow, orange, or blended combinations of the same tones will often stimulate strikes from seatrout. Other popular colors are root beer, motor oil, red, white, and lime green. Flies that replicate shrimp, small crustaceans, and small baitfish perform best. Specks will also respond well to topwater flies and bugs.

Atlantic Bonito (*Sarda sarda*)

Atlantic bonito can be found in the temperate and tropical waters of the Atlantic Ocean. The species is present along the entire East Coast. While many bonito are caught offshore from boats, they do present numerous opportunities for fly anglers fishing from shore. In the Northeast, bonito are often referred to as "bones"; in the Southeast they're called green bonito, to distinguish them from little tunny, which are often referred to as bonito or bonita.

Atlantic bonito are members of the same family of fish as mackerel, tuna, and their sometime traveling companions, false albacore. They are speedsters that at times can be observed jumping or skipping along the surface of the water while in pursuit of baitfish. Bonito also have a mouth of distinctive dentures that are more than capable of handling larger baitfish. They are not at all shy about eating large fly patterns. Due to their surface-feeding activity, bonito also attract the attention of terns and gulls, as do feeding schools of bluefish. Often, just a few terns will be on

Atlantic bonito.

the fast-moving and leaping pods of bonito, unlike the extensive bird activity that takes place over huge schools of bluefish. Bonito can be finicky feeders and difficult to hook, but they readily take flies and will offer opportunities to the patient wading angler.

One telltale characteristic of bonito is a series of dark lateral bars running along the upper portions of their flanks, including the shoulder and back areas. These lines run in contrast to dark bars that flow vertically along the shoulders. The general coloration of bonito is an iridescent blue-green hue with a dark back and a mottled white to silvery lower flank region and belly. When first caught, bonito light up with an almost neon quality.

One of the critical elements for a sustained bonito run is the presence of large Atlantic silversides, or other moderate-size whitebait. The best Northeast runs of bonito appear to track coincidentally with the presence of large schools of big spearing. While bonito feed on peanut bunker, bay anchovies, sand eels, and other small baitfish, or rainbait, they consistently show a marked preference for spearing. During a recent season, a large number of bonito entered the waters of Long Island and zoned in on an equally sizable mass of big spearing, some of which were in excess of five inches in length. The silversides found conditions conducive to sticking around for an unusually extended period of time, and the bonito followed suit. Those "bones" remained for more than two months, providing anglers with numerous shots at them daily both from boats and from the beach. Although an ocean-roaming species, when preferred bait is available, bonito will often show consistently inshore and close to beaches in numbers that allow for terrific fly-rod sport. Find the bait and locate suitable water temperatures, and chances are good for enjoying an extended bonito season, long after others have given them up for gone.

Bonito are schooling fish, so find one and there will be plenty more around, usually in the form of small pods or groupings that work in concert to corral and push bait to the surface, a trait that is quite beneficial to the fly fisherman. The standard flyfishing method for bonito involves mostly visual observation of feeding fish. Their tendency to leap from the water after prey is often the giveaway to their presence. Also, diving birds following pods of bonito around are another indicator of activity. It is the speed of bonito that presents the real challenge to surf fly fishermen. The fly angler fishing from shore should attempt to determine the feeding direction of the pod or school, and try to intercept that path. When the fish surface, make a quick, accurate cast, ahead of and in a manner that will have the fly pass in front of the feeding fish. Retrieves can vary, but one of the more popular methods is the double overhand retrieve—stripping line with one hand, then the other, at a rapid pace. A stripping basket comes in handy when retrieving in this fashion. I've found that getting the fly into motion quickly is often a key to hook-up success when targeting surface-feeding bonito.

Bonito, like most other predators, are opportunists and readily take the easy pickings as well. After a pod of "bones" slashes through baitfish, they sometimes remain in the area to pick up the remnants of the carnage—injured and stunned baitfish. I've often watched injured spearing—victims of bonito blitzes—flutter slowly down in the water, only to be snatched from their free fall by a supercharged bonito materializing from the depths. Bonito hang around to capitalize on these easy meals, and as such a "do-nothing" retrieve will often work well. After the initial casting to breaking fish, allow the fly to simply descend, with minimal retrieving action. Every once in a while during the descent, move the fly ever so slowly, as if it were an injured or stunned baitfish attempting to regain its stability. When employing this technique, it pays to have a fly that displays flash while fluttering down and to use a higher-density sink tip. I make it a point to keep a rod rigged with a sinking tip or sinking line at the ready for just these situations.

Catching bonito by wading is a tough proposition since they move so quickly, but it can be done with a reasonable degree of consistency and success. The best approach for this type of fishing is to select an area along the beach that bonito are known to frequent and just hang out there. The game from the surf takes patience and some good fortune. Try to position yourself in such a way so as to be close to areas where the bonito corral the bait— points, eddies, and areas of swiftly moving current. Bonito also pursue bait in areas of calm water as well.

Little Tunny (*Euthynnus alletteratus*)

The arrival of false albacore to the waters of the mid-Atlantic and Northeast states is an eagerly awaited migratory event. While present in large numbers in the Southeast, a wealth of other preferred species has kept attention off this gamester, but interest has grown in this species as a formidable flyfishing adversary. Northern anglers wait all season for this pelagic member of the mackerel and tuna family to finally show its fins. It is a veritable torpedo of a fish and one of the finest fly-rod species to roam the Atlantic. Albies will test your casting skills, your fly selection, and your patience. It is an especially humbling fish when pursued from the surf.

Referred to endearingly by fly rodders as albies, fat Alberts, hardtails, false albacore, and little tunny, this is one of the most coveted of all Northeast gamefish. Anglers in the Southeast refer to the species as "bonita." The little tunny is a wide-ranging species. It can be found in the waters of the Atlantic Ocean from Florida to New England. It is also prevalent in the waters of Brazil, Bermuda, and from South Africa to Great Britain to the Mediterranean Sea. A false albacore is a stout, strongly built fish that is easily identified by its unique markings. One of the most distinguishing features of the species is a pattern of vermiculations, wormlike blotches high on the back. Albies also have telltale black markings or large dots located between the pectoral and ventral fins.

Schooling albies consistently frequent harbors, inlets, shoals, tidal pond outflows, and offshore areas, and thus give the shore and surf angler many opportunities to engage. It is a remarkable sight seeing false albacore herding bay anchovies

Little tunny.

into tight quarters in quiet backwaters, and then systematically assaulting them. Any configuration of structure that causes currents and tide to move in such a way as to tumble bait about is a potential area of opportunity. In the Northeast, late August through October are the best months for consistent albie action from the beach. October and November see solid action in the mid-Atlantic region, and availability in the Southeast runs throughout most of the year.

When the albie game is on, the fly angler can literally cast into acres or surface-breaking fish, often close enough to shore to give fly anglers many shots at hook-ups. Since albies move about quickly, this can become a very intense and frenzied affair. I have had many encounters with beach albies where sprinting up and down the beach exhausted an entire day. But patience pays when fishing for these speedsters. Like bonito, albies will continue to circulate within an area after the initial busting of bait, remaining to feed on the stunned and injured prey, so it is also productive at these times to use sinking tips and lines to allow the fly to flutter down, occasionally giving the fly some subtle action. This tactic works quite well when fishing from jetties.

While in the fury of surface feeding, albies respond well to a fast hand-over-hand retrieve using clear-tip intermediate or floating lines. Effective line control and line management are imperative to successful hook-ups; a stripping basket for storing line helps immensely with this. When a fish takes, a combination strip set and rod lift work well in tandem to drive the hook home.

Many of the same fishing techniques described for bonito are effective for false albacore. One notable difference when fly fishing for albies is that they seem to have a fondness for smaller baits and therefore smaller flies. Bay anchovies, any form of rainbait, and small spearing are preferred. There are times when albies get extremely selective, particularly when they are zoned in on diminutive baits. That is usually when the fishing is at its most frustrating level. Yet there are also times when they feed indiscriminately on larger bait and eat whatever fly you might toss at them. One of the biggest challenges the surf fly angler faces when casting to fall-run albies that are feasting on masses of anchovies is getting the fly noticed. Therefore it is sometimes an effective tactic to go against the flow, and show the fish a fly that stands out from the pack of bait, a distinctly different profile and form. For me, this means bigger and flashier flies—attention grabbers. While this approach doesn't always work, I've had enough success with it to keep it in my tool bag of albie tricks.

Spanish Mackerel (*Scomberomorus maculatus*)

Spanish mackerel are usually considered more of a tropical and temperate zone species, but they do make brief seasonal visits to Northeast waters where they are more of a secondary fly-rod species, since their arrival and stay are not always consistent or dependable. They are most often found in the Northeast as a bycatch

Spanish mackerel.   (Photo credit: Nick Angelo)

for inshore anglers fishing for bonito and false albacore, since mackerel will relate to similar habitats and conditions. The populations of Spanish mackerel that inhabit the Southeast are more prolific and more available to fly anglers than those that migrate north. Their complete range embraces the geography from Mexico's Yucatan Peninsula to Cape Cod, Massachusetts. As water temperatures rise along the Atlantic coast, Spanish mackerel migrate from the Florida Keys up to Cape Cod, and then return south in the fall. Other migratory groupings of Spanish mackerel move in patterns that take them to the west coast of Florida and through the Gulf states.

The primary body characteristics of Spanish mackerel are silvery flanks, a green back, and numerous elliptical body spots. Females of the species are the larger of the two sexes and can attain impressive size. The two largest (IGFA) Spanish mackerel taken on flies were both caught in Massachusetts and weighed in at identically the same weight: eight pounds, eleven ounces.

In relative terms, Spanish mackerel are a shallow-water species and have a preference for sand bottoms in ten to forty feet of water. Regardless of where they are caught, "macks" are wonderful treats for the fly rodder since they readily strike flies. They are aggressive schooling fish with an impressive set of sharp dentures. Mackerel show by and large in the Northeast during August and most often appear offshore, near inlets and promontories, and will occasionally divert well into bays, harbors, and sounds. The can also be caught from piers, jetties, and beaches. The strength and duration of their Northeast visits directly correlate with the warming of local water temperatures and available bait.

At times I've literally stumbled upon a pod of surface-feeding mackerel while fishing from the beach for false albacore and bonito. The mackerel were mixed in with the albies and bluefish and had spearing packed in a tight ball. A fly cast into the melee resulted in a quick hook-up with a mackerel that pushed the scale to seven pounds. Spanish mackerel have a mouthful of impressive teeth that enable them to prey on moderate-sized baits. Their dietary preferences include many varieties of small baitfish like peanut bunker, anchovies, alewives, and herring. Spanish mackerel will also consume shrimp and squid. Most beach-fishing techniques and flies that are effective for bonito and albies are also productive for Spanish mackerel.

Hickory Shad (*Alosa mediocris*)

Hickory shad are fly fishing's somewhat forgotten gamefish. Yet many anglers have enjoyed fine days of hickory shad fishing while wading after early season striped bass. A close cousin of the American shad, hickory shad are more often caught in salt water and brackish water; sport fishing for American shad is most often associated with freshwater rivers. The full extent of the hickory shad range is similar to that of other anadromous East Coast species and includes the entire seaboard, from Florida to Maine. The largest concentrations of fish are located within the midportions of that range, from Maryland to North Carolina. Hickory shad are fundamentally a shallow-water species that roams close to shore.

Hickory shad.

In the northern latitudes, hickories makes an annual appearance sometime in late April or early May. The hickory shad, like its American relative, has inherited some of the same traits of its oversized herring family member, the tarpon. Hickory shad must think like big fish in small fish bodies, for they aggressively hit flies, jump, and pull harder pound for pound than any stocked freshwater trout. Hickories are a migratory species that travel in schools. These shad feed on a wide range of bait including small spearing and other baitfish, krill, shrimp, and various diminutive crustaceans. The hickory shad's coloration is gray-green along the back, with silvery flanks and grayish shoulders. The hickory also has several dark spots along its sides and sawlike scales along its underside. One of the most distinguishing features of hickory shad is the prominent and protruding lower jaw.

When fished on appropriately matched fly tackle, the hickory shad will give a good accounting of itself. Big roe American shad can reach weights of eight or nine pounds; bucks are about half that size. By comparison, hickories are half the size of the Americans—an exceptional roe fish can be four pounds, a buck fish around two pounds. They are active in our waters most heavily from late spring until the end of June. Shad prefer cooler water temperatures and become active inshore with water around the mid-fifties and into sixty-degree temperatures. While they can still be found in summer months, spring is by far the peak time.

When fly fishing for shad from the surf, lighter outfits perform well. Any good trout rod in 6- or 7-weight is ideal; no need to go much larger than an 8-weight. Even if school-sized striped bass are in the neighborhood, the lighter rods offer much more enjoyment. Since shad feed on a wide array of food sources, from plankton to small crustacean and baitfish, a number of different flies work quite well. Small versions of Deceivers and Clouser Minnows are ideal, but I have found that tiny, dart-size flies used for sockeye salmon work very well in all sorts of wild colors: chartreuse, orange, gold, yellow, and red are some personal favorites. Any number of small, colorful flies will entice shad to strike. Crazy Charlies in bright color combinations are very effective for shad. As far as lines go, preferences are toward high-density sink-tip lines. A short, four- to six-foot leader is all that is required, since shad are far from being line shy. Shad can also be fished effectively on light spinning gear.

Look for shad in the early season from about late April through June and then again in the fall months. Often they are in many of the same locations where striped bass are found: rock outcroppings, riprap, jetties, harbor entrances, rips, and long eddies adjacent to points.

Summer Flounder/Fluke (*Paralichthys dentatus*)

Fluke or summer flounder are fast becoming a regularly targeted fly-rod species. These flatfish can be caught consistently on flies from both boat and the surf.

According to the IGFA record book, the largest tippet class record fluke caught on a fly weighed in at eight pounds, four ounces and was taken from the waters of Cape May, New Jersey. Fluke are a prolific species with a wide range. They can be found primarily from Maine to South Carolina. Within that geography, it is one of the most sought-after gamefish. In the Northeast and mid-Atlantic states, it is second in the popularity polls only to striped bass. Fluke are one of the most easily identified of all fish species. The fish has a distinctly white underbelly, with a dark brown, mottled, and spotted back, and eyes positioned on the top of its head. Unlike their closest relative, the winter flounder, fluke have notable mouths full of sharp teeth. This enables fluke to deal with larger prey ranging from big sand eels and spearing to squid. Fluke burrow in the sand and remain motionless until some unsuspecting prey moves into their feeding zone. When prey reach the strike zone, fluke accelerate out from the sand and attack with surprising speed and accuracy. Fluke are very aggressive feeders and also follow bait for some distance before striking. Almost all fluke anglers have experienced situations where fish follow a baited rig as it is being retrieved and then ultimately strike the bait at the surface. Fluke also pursue a fly in similar fashion.

The fact that fluke will readily strike flies in the surf may come as a surprise to some fly anglers, but more and more surf fishermen are beginning to intentionally target them with flies. Most initial encounters with fluke on the fly rod occur by chance—a byproduct of early season striped bass fishing in the shallower back-bay

Summer flounder. (Photo credit: Chris Paparo)

areas, either from the beach or boat. That is how it was with my first fly-rod fluke. I had been fishing a sandy beach adjacent to a mud flat when my sand eel pattern was stopped solidly during the retrieve. As I strip set the fly and lifted the rod, I felt a most gratifying weight on the end of my line. Expecting to see a school striped bass, I was surprised when a keeper-sized fluke surfaced with the fly just barely visible within its mouth. From that point forward I have made it an objective to specifically seek out summer flatties during early season outings, and I always expect to catch a few on flies under similar spring conditions.

The most productive habitat from which to tempt a fly-rod fluke is shallow water over a sandy bottom. Back bays and harbors are ideal places to find early season fluke. These situations are perfect for the wading fly angler. In these environs, their strikes often come several rods lengths away, right off the beach, but they can also be caught on a fly rod in deeper water. When fishing from the beach, an 8-weight rod is usually adequate for fluke when matched to an intermediate or high-density sink tip. When fishing areas with current, the preference is for a 9-weight, not so much for the size of the fish but rather for handling higher-density sink tips or full-sinking lines.

A sandy shoal where bait and fluke congregate can be an especially productive area to prospect with the fly rod. If the shoal is adjacent to deeper water, there will often be some larger fluke on the prowl. Some of the most productive fly-rod fluke locations are expansive sand flats that are in close proximity to deep water.

Water with a depth beyond fifteen or twenty feet really becomes impractical as a venue for the fly rod. In most instances when fishing for fluke the fly is cast and then allowed to sink, utilizing the full length of an extended sink tip and running line or the entire length of a sinking line. Getting the fly as close to the bottom as possible, and keeping it there, is imperative. The sinking fly line does all the work, perhaps aided by either a small conehead sinker or a barbell sinker. If the drift is too fast or the water movement too strong, the fly line will remain suspended most of the time out of the prime fluke zone. Once the fly has descended, it is important to stay in touch with the fly line and maintain constant contact with the fly.

Wading for fluke is especially productive the early part of the season when the fluke are predisposed to shallow water. Again, the best strategy is to concentrate on backwater areas, bays, and mud and sand flats. The downtide edges of protruding sandbars are also productive areas to seek out. My preference is to wade, walk, and cast until I happen upon a receptive fluke or two, then I focus my efforts on those specific holding areas. Casting from the surf allows one to use intermediate or low sink rate fly lines, with 8-weight rods a good all-around choice.

The most productive fluke flies are variations of the Clouser Deep Minnow and the Popovics Jiggy. Any number of other small weighted flies that give the impression of a tiny bucktail jig also work well. These types of patterns are successful due to the inherent jigging motion that occurs upon both the descent and the retrieve. This action draws attention and, given their weighted construction, aids in keeping them closer to the bottom and in the fluke zone longer. In shallower water, the weighted heads can kick up little puffs of sand that act as attention grabbers, especially when sand eels are present. Flies can be weighted with the addition of conehead or barbell eyes tied in on the shank in the area of the hook eye. A double set of barbells can be tied in for additional weight. When fishing off the beach, it is beneficial to tie such weight in on the top of the shank so as to allow the hook point to ride up, Clouser-style. This minimizes snagging and the dulling of the hook point as it is pulled through sandy areas. For me the most effective color combinations for fluke have been chartreuse over white with the addition of blended yellow and olive and some flash material; yellow and red combinations have also produced good results. I prefer natural materials such as bucktail or small to midsize saddle hackles, but synthetics also work well. Sand eel patterns are especially effective for fluke, as are spearing and small squid flies. Preferably, the fly should be cast up-current and allowed to drift naturally and as close to the bottom as is practicable; retrieves should be slow. When the line starts to come tight or if a subtle pause is felt, strip set the fly while raising the rod. Often the aggressiveness of the fluke will result in an unmistakable hit. It is also advisable to use a shock tippet, since a fluke's teeth will shred a lesser leader.

Redfish (*Sciaenops ocellatus*)

Whether they're referred to as red drum, channel bass, spot tail bass, or any other colloquial name, there is no question that redfish are superb fly-rod fish that can be caught readily when wading. The primary range of redfish extends from the southern portions of the mid-Atlantic regions, through the Southeast and the entire Gulf Coast. Redfish can be found in a variety of settings, from shallow sand and mud flats to grass expanses, marshes, coastal beaches, backcountry, and bays. Small reds are often referred to as rats, while those over twenty-eight inches or so are called bull reds.

Redfish prey predominantly on all varieties of crustaceans, small fish and a wide range of mollusks. As opportunistic feeders, they will regularly eat shrimp, whitebait, and crabs. While they will often feed at various levels of the water column, redfish prefer to feed in proximity to the bottom, where they root for all forms of food sources. Redfish have a somewhat downward-angled bull-nose snout that facilitates this sort of feeding behavior. As a result, flies fished on or near the bottom are very effective.

Redfish sport a copper or bronze coloration with tints of red on silver and gray flanks. Their backs are colored with dark red tones that transition to a typically white

Redfish. (Photo credit: Rich Santos)

underbelly. The most readily identifiable markings on redfish are their spots. There will typically be an eye-shaped spot in the tail region. Evolutionary biologists would suggest that this marking worked to distract predators from attacking the fish's head and rather bite at the tail. Some redfish have many such markings scattered about their bodies. Redfish grow to impressive size. The current IGFA all-tackle record was caught in North Carolina and stands at ninety-four pounds, two ounces; the largest redfish taken on a fly is currently recorded at forty-three pounds and was caught in the Banana River Lagoon, Florida.

The most challenging and fulfilling way for a fly angler to catch reds is by wading after fish feeding in shallow water in a manner referred to as tailing. This behavior occurs when redfish use their snouts to probe for bottom-dwelling food. As they move about rooting, their tails break through the surface of the shallow water, often glistening in the sun. When engaged in that form of feeding activity over mud flats, small puffs of mud will usually indicate the presence of reds. Either form of feeding presents a challenging fly casting opportunity.

My indoctrination to wading after tailing redfish came about in southwest Florida during a fishing outing that began on the casting platform of a flats skiff. The boat came to a halt about 100 yards from an expansive sand flat, and was then quietly poled the remaining distance to the edge of the flat. The sun was high, providing the best visual opportunity to spot fish. Within minutes redfish were spotted feeding and I spied the first glimmering tail of a mudding red. Readying myself on the bow, I held the brown and purple fly at the ready for a quick cast. Once within casting range, the small imitation crustacean was cast to the right of the fish's head, as its snout was preoccupied rooting in the sand for the next meal. The fish didn't take nor did it spook. It just moved slowly away. Despite seeing other active tails on the flat we chose to pursue that specific fish, and I did get to make several more frustrating and fruitless presentations. After the last of those casts I decided to leave the boat and wade, figuring that would offer a quieter approach. I followed that individual redfish for about thirty minutes until it took a position that allowed me to make a number of close casts, trying all the while to be as stealthy as a heron. After many refusals, and for some reason known only to the fish, it finally decided to eat. One short strip elicited the solid take. My fishing companion let out with a whoop as the red took off toward the deep edge of the flat. I held on and after an enjoyable tussle slid my hand under the belly of a gratifying 30-inch Pine Island Sound redfish—the first of a few that we caught that morning. That experience fueled a passion for sight casting flies to redfish while wading.

Snook (*Centropomus undecimalis*)

Snook are common to the coastal waters of Florida, the region of the Texas Gulf Coast, and the waters of Central and South America. Snook are one of the most exciting gamefish fly anglers can catch from the surf or from backcountry areas. Also known as robalo, common snook are predisposed to take up residence in estuaries, around mangrove islands, lagoons, inshore coastal areas, and other shallow water

Snook. (Photo credit: Marcia Foosaner)

locations. Snook are also tolerant of brackish water and will often transition into fresh water. Their receptivity to strike flies, and their sporting qualities, not the least of which are fighting and leaping prowess, make snook one of the most sought-after of the inshore species of gamefish. They are also one of the most exciting fish to catch when wading the surf.

A snook's body coloration is relatively plain with the exception of a prominent black lateral line and yellow caudal and pelvic fins. The snout is pike-like. The female of the species is the larger of the sexes, reaching lengths of about forty-eight inches. Males are known to reaches sizes of approximately forty inches. There are no distinct differences between the sexes, so identification via observation is difficult. As a matter of fact, snook are biologically considered protandric hermaphrodites; the males are capable of changing into females. The current IGFA all-tackle record is fifty-three pounds, ten ounces, and the largest snook taken on a fly was caught at Chockoloskee Island, Florida, tipping the scales at thirty pounds, four ounces. Snook will prey upon any number of small fishes, crustaceans, crabs, and their favorite food source, shrimp.

Snook for the most part are relative homebodies, and do not normally venture far from their primary habitat. The one exception to this behavior is during spawning season when snook move from their wintering areas to their spawning grounds. This migration typically occurs in late spring and early summer. Snook relate well to many forms of structure that are accessible to surf fly anglers. They can be found around jetties, bridge abutments, inlets, passes, flats, channels, cuts, sandbars, mangrove islands, docks, and ocean- or gulf-facing beaches. Many of these configurations are well within reach of the wading angler.

One of the most enjoyable and fulfilling ways to fly fish for snook is along shoreline beaches, sight casting to cruising fish. These fish will often be mere feet or inches from the edge of the shoreline searching for a meal. Use the sun as your ally and wear a good pair of polarized sunglasses to aid in spotting fish. I have a preference for a receding tide but incoming water can yield fine results as well. As with most inshore gamefish, finding and fishing areas where there is current is usually more important than tide phase. Once you spot a cruising snook, future identification is easy; the fish will appear as dark, elongated forms. Successful hook-ups usually require a cast that places the fly ahead of the cruising snook in a manner that allows the fish to intercept the offering in a natural way. Try as well not to cast your own shadow upon the water; fish that frequent the shallows to feed will be very wary of any such silhouette due to an imprinted fear of airborne predators. Snook will move away from such potential threats, but often will cycle back to the same area. I once walked up and down the same stretch of beach for almost forty-five minutes, pursuing the same snook. It never really spooked, just moved away and then moved back.

As with most other forms of sight fishing, the best conditions for catching snook in this manner require clear and somewhat calm waters and bright skies to maximize visibility. Although the objective of this game is to cast flies to fish the angler can see, very often snook may cruise within casting range yet their presence won't be evident to the angler. When fish aren't showing it pays to fan-cast an area, first close to the edges along the beach, and then outward in a semicircular progression. If you can identify a trough in the surf zone, cast parallel to that structure, both up and down the beach from your position. Remain on the sand while casting, since snook may be in the surf zone even though they are not visible. Entering the water prematurely will spook the fish. Surf-zone structure like sandbars, points, troughs, and potholes will also attract and hold snook. In backcountry areas, mangrove islands, or shorelines containing mangroves or other cover, are also areas of preference for snook. There is something very special about casting flies tight up against or into mangroves and watching the big white maw of a snook move to engulf the offering.

Bonefish (*Albula vulpes*)

Bonefish are the poster fish of the flats. What immediately comes to mind when "bones" are mentioned are sand flats, stealthy approaches, sizzling runs, and screaming drags. Bonefish live their lives in inshore tropical waters. In addition to their physical attributes, they appeal to the fly angler because of a disposition to travel onto shallow and wadable sand or mudflats to feed. Bonefish will move onto those flats with the incoming tide and slide back into deeper water as the tide recedes. During periods of thin water, bonefish can be observed feeding by watching exposed tail or caudal fins, or small puffs of mud or sand as the fish root about the

Bonefish.   (Photo credit: Jason Puris)

bottom for food. Due to their silvery and gray coloration, bonefish can often be difficult to see, especially when cruising on a flat with higher water. This trait gives rise to the moniker Phantom of the Flats. One of the largest bonefish I've caught was seen first by the trained eye of the guide who, at the time, was perched high upon a poling platform. I eventually got to see the fish about sixty feet out, as it passed over a piece of dark bottom. The challenge when wading increases substantially, since the cone of observation is smaller when the angler is at the water's level as opposed to being elevated on a boat's casting platform. That makes stealthy wading and visual acuity very important, and polarized sunglasses mandatory.

Bonefish can be found in water from six inches to a few feet in depth, where they will root about the bottom for food. They will typically travel in large schools or small pods. The largest schools will usually be comprised of juvenile specimens while the largest bonefish will travel in small pods or as single cruisers. Any of these configurations present unique challenges for the wading angler. When approaching a large school of small bonefish the angler is confronted with multiple sets of eyes and many nervous bodies. An errant cast will blow up the entire school and send them fleeing. Here are two observations from personal experience. Fish the edges of the school, and cast to select fish rather than the entire school. It is much like flushing a covey of quail. If you shoot at the entire body of birds you almost guarantee a miss. Pick one out and stay with it. Also, if you stay put after busting those juvenile bonefish, the school just may cycle back to where they were, giving you another and hopefully more controlled shot. Larger bones rely on their accumulated experience and will be as wary as fish can be. You get bit of a break when they are preoccupied while mudding, but even then angle the cast and put it somewhat off to the side. A fly line landing on or over the fish will result in game over.

Bonefish prefer a diet consisting of shrimp, crabs, other crustaceans, small baitfish, worms, and mollusks. Unquestionably, some of the most effective bonefish flies replicate small- to moderate-sized shrimp and crabs. Some of the largest bonefish are caught on crab, creature, and critter flies.

Permit (*Trachinotus falcatus*)

While bonefish are the poster fish of the flats, permit are the glamour fish of skinny-water fly fishing. Many argue that permit represent the apex of saltwater sight fishing. They may be right. Beyond question, the permit is universally recognized as one of the most challenging fly-rod species to roam the waters of the Southeast and Gulf Coast. The permit is a deep-bodied fish with a trademark scythe-shaped dorsal fin, long anal fin, and deep forked tail. Like bonefish, permit are found in tropical aquatic habitats and prefer shallow sand and mud flats and adjacent troughs and channels. Permit will characteristically travel in small pods or as single fish and will move

Permit. (Photo credit: Chris Paparo)

about at a slow to moderate pace. This tendency presents some casting and fishing challenges for the fly angler. First and foremost, most permit caught on the flats are done so from the casting platform of a skiff. Smaller permit will frequent shallow areas along the surf line while larger fish will prefer offshore flats, channels, and troughs.

When there is an opportunity to get in the water and wade after permit, the stakes get higher. Not only are permit very cautious fish, spooked easily by casting errors or careless wading, but the angler needs to spot cruising fish. This takes some learning. Just as a hunter learns to look for parts of a well-concealed animal rather than looking for the whole animal, so it is with permit. Most successful permit anglers learn to distinguish the dark, forked tail as a key to the orientation of permit. As with bonefish, permit that are feeding and tailing make for somewhat easier targets. Yet, success at the game requires casting accuracy. Conventional wisdom suggests that a close cast often works well on a tailing/feeding fish, while leading a permit is mandatory for a cruising fish. Crabs are far and away the favorite food for permit and, as such, flies that replicate these crustaceans are a top choice for fly anglers. One of the flies that revolutionized fly fishing for permit is Del Brown's Merkin Crab. True to the origins of its name, the "merkin" is deceptively effective when presented to permit in a natural, free-falling way. The perfect permit crab fly is balanced to descend the water column as a live crab, scurrying to seek sanctuary on the bottom. If the cast is on the mark and if the permit sees it and responds, the fly will often be eaten on the fall, without any additional manipulation. Should the fly be ignored, a few tempting strips of line can be used to impart subtle action to the fly. If there is still no interest and the permit is still in the neighborhood, wait until the fly hits bottom and then strip to create a small puff of sand or mud. There are many terrific crab fly patterns around these days and most have originated to fool wary permit. While this a far from an easy game, it is certainly one of the most rewarding of all flyfishing pursuits.

Tarpon (*Megalops atlanticus*)

A number of years back, I received a call from a cousin of mine living in Florida telling me he had hooked and jumped nine small- to medium-sized tarpon in a morning of fly fishing. I congratulated him and asked when he bought a boat. He said he didn't. The tarpon were hooked from shore as they congregated near jetty and dock structure. I received subsequent calls from my cousin over the next few days that reported similar results. By the time his private stash of 'poons moved on, he had tallied an impressive fifty-four hook-ups. While the majority of those hooked fish bid him adieu after taking flight, he did manage to land several. Needless to say, I coveted my cousin's good fortune.

The overwhelming majority of tarpon are taken from boats and those who regularly catch tarpon from the surf at night do so with bait and artificial lures. Tarpon will frequent areas accessible to wading anglers: beaches, passes, docks, bridges, and jetties.

Consistently catching tarpon on a fly from the beach is a formidable challenge but it can be done. Success at this game requires a resolute will, patience, and unyielding determination; success is often measured in small victories. The challenge is to place the fly in the path of oncoming fish, often moving at high rates of speed across open sand and grass flats. The fly must be presented at a correct angle so that

Tarpon.   (Photo credit: Nick Angelo)

it crosses the path of the tarpon in a natural way. This involves leading fish with the cast, much as a quarterback leads a receiver. Despite their size, tarpon are surprisingly wary of anything—including flies—that comes at them from an unnatural direction. Once the fly is cast and allowed to sink to the level of the fish, long, steady retrieves should get it to intersect the fish's route and capture its attention. Should the fish react to the fly in a positive way, chalk that up as a minor victory.

When a big tarpon tracks a fly in thin water it is tough to maintain one's composure while watching the drama unfold! I can vouch for that from personal experience. Buck fever pales in comparison to this deal! But the fly must continue moving along steadily and in a way so as to maintain the "beast's" interest. Sometimes, tarpon will nose the fly or bump it. This is when one's self control needs be at its peak. Often, a break in the retrieve with either a slight pause or some form of subtle seduction—like jiggling the fly with the rod tip—can excite and stimulate the fish. The goal at this stage of the presentation is to make the fly look alive—to get the tarpon to want to eat it. If the fish actually does inhale the fly, consider that another minor victory, or perhaps even a small miracle!

When a tarpon does eat, one of two things will happen. The strike will either be an unmistakable, bone-jarring smash, or a take so subtle you will think a small seatrout may have mouthed the fly. This latter strike is where it gets tricky. The natural inclination is to lift the rod. That is a big mistake! I've been there, too! At this point in the game, one needs to keep the fly in motion, even if you see the take and the accompanying flash of a turning fish. The key is letting the line go completely tight, as if you were hung up on a log. Once that happens, a few strip strikes just might seal the deal. If the fly angler makes it this far, congratulations on a job well done. But the mission is far from accomplished, for this is when the difficult work begins in fighting the fish and getting it to the beach.

The potential scope of surf fly fishing is limited only by the imagination and creativity of the angler. The general presumption is that if a particular species of fish can be caught using traditional surf-fishing methods, it can also be caught on flies. Not surprisingly, assorted and sundry species have been caught on the fly. When conditions are conducive, the following popular species are regularly caught very close to shore and on flies. While the species profiled above are the premier fly-rod gamefish, the ones that follow below are worthy targets of opportunity that will provide many fulfilling outings for wading anglers.

Jack Crevalle (*Caranx hippos*)

The first time I caught a large Jack Crevalle on a fly I remember thinking, these things are like bluefish on steroids. I was fishing a beach in southwest Florida

Jacks (Photo credit: Chris Paparo)

when I encountered a small school of big jacks within casting range of the fly rod. They were circling tight around some hapless baitfish. A slim white and chartreuse Deceiver cast smack dab in the middle of the fish brought an instant strike. I hung around those fish the entire morning, wanting more of the same, and temporarily forgetting about the snook that I intended to target. Jacks of all sizes are fun and are not too discriminate about the flies they will hit, so a wide variety of patterns will work.

Ladyfish (*Elops saurus*)

No other species of Southeast gamefish has saved the day for me more than ladyfish. While at times they can appear as an annoyance when sights are set on loftier fish, there are those times that their presence and willingness to strike a fly is welcomed. Ladyfish will strike flies aggressively and, relative to their body length, will make impressive leaps from the water and skip along the surface. Ladyfish can grow to about a maximum of three feet in length and the current IGFA all-tackle record is eight pounds. Most of the ladyfish caught on flies range between one and four pounds. Their size belies their aggressiveness: tarpon traits, in a small body. This exciting and fun fish will indiscriminately strike at most any fly that imitates small baitfish.

Ladyfish.   (Photo credit: Rich Santos)

Sheepshead (*Archosargus probatocephalus*)

I once entertained myself for the better part of a morning casting flies to sheepshead that were cruising along a shallow shelf near the beach line. I had tired of casting a fly to rather large and uninterested snook and figured these small, striped convict fish would be easier targets. Wrong! Sheepshead can be more challenging than bonefish to hook on flies. While they will readily take bait, it seems they have to be in the right mood to eat a well-placed and manipulated fly. Sheepshead can be found along the beach line, nestled in mangrove roots, around docks, piers, rock piles, and jetties. Their dietary preferences include small shrimp, crabs, mollusks,

Sheepshead.   (Photo credit: Nick Angelo)

and baitfish. Shrimp and crab flies are the best choices for these fish. Sheepshead can grow to about twenty pounds, but will typically range between one and six pounds for the fly angler.

Tautog (*Tautoga onitis*)

Blackfish are prized for their flesh and for their bulldog fighting style. They are most often caught on cut crab baits fished among deepwater structure. In the spring and early fall, 'tog will move inshore and will come within reach of shore-bound fly casters. Blackfish will relate to many forms of inshore structures like rock piles, jetties, piers, boat docks, and depressions close to shore. Since crustaceans are the tautog's main food preference, crab flies are the best choice. Blackfish are bottom feeders and as such flies should be fished on a full sinking line or a long, high-density sink tip. While it may seem like heresy to flyfishing purists, a little dab of liquid crab scent applied to the crab fly will improve bites. Blackfish will often nibble at bait, so give them time to taste, nibble, and eat the fly before setting the hook. A stout fly rod should be used since the first reaction of a 'tog after being hooked is to head into cover. They are difficult to hook on flies but it is not impossible.

Tautog.   (Photo credit: Chris Paparo)

Scup. (Photo credit: Chris Paparo)

Scup (*Stenotomus chrysops*)

Better known as porgies, these small gamesters are the perennial "panfish of the Northeast coast." When they frequent shallow water, show them a small Clouser or Jiggy-style fly and they will strike. And after they eat the fly, prepare yourself for a fun fight, especially if you hook into a large humpback porgy. Scup are present in a wide range of the Atlantic from Massachusetts to South Carolina; the greatest concentrations of scup occur within the middle regions of the Northeast and mid-Atlantic zones. The majority of porgies are in the one-half- to one-pound range, with the largest weighing three to four pounds. Small, bright flies work well. My personal preference is a chartreuse over white Clouser Deep Minnow. I've also had success with red and yellow patterns.

Pompano (*Trachinotus carolinus*)

The Florida pompano is another terrific inshore species to catch on a fly. This compact member of the jack family will weigh in on average at about three pounds or less and reach a top weight of nine pounds. Its compressed body shape is somewhat permit-like, with a deep, forked

Pompano   (Photo credit: Marcia Foosaner)

tail and a prominent rounded snout. Pompano will frequent the surf zone and flats, and will travel about in schools. Early summer through the fall months produce excellent fishing for pompano. Since the species feeds on the bottom, intermediate sink tips will work well in shallow water. Chartreuse and white and yellow and white Clouser Deep Minnows will get the job done.

Atlantic Croaker (*Micropogonias undulatus*)

This prolific member of the drum family can provide some active shallow-water fly fishing. Croaker are also related to weakfish, redfish, and seatrout, and can be regularly caught from the surf, back bays, estuaries, inlets, jetties, and piers. They feed on shrimp, crabs, other crustaceans, worms, and a variety of bottom-dwelling baits. Clousers, small baitfish patterns, and small crab flies work well. Inshore croakers will range between one and two pounds. For their size, croakers are tenacious and will give a solid fight on suitably matched fly tackle. What they lack in bulk, they make up in quantity, traveling in schools that can at times be quite large. Croaker are named for the sound they emit when taken from the water.

Croaker.   (Photo credit: Rich Santos)

Chapter Eight

The Bait and the Flies

Baitfish, crabs, shrimp, crustaceans, and other forms of marine food sources that gamefish feed upon are at the core of saltwater fly fishing. Without those baits there would be no need for flies to imitate a potential meal. That may be stating the obvious, but having an intimate and working knowledge of seasonal habitat and habits of bait is critical to the success of any surf fly angler. All the successful saltwater fly fishermen I know spend as much time understanding the movements, habits, and tendencies of bait as they do similar patterns of the gamefish they pursue. This knowledge is especially relevant when fishing the surf zone or other shallow water areas. The importance of bait in the flyfishing equation is analogous to a three-legged stool supported by three elements: bait, moving water in the form of tides or current, and fish-holding structure. Comprehending and applying those components to one's fly fishing will undoubtedly increase an angler's success ratio. Congregations and movements of bait vary with the seasons and with water temperature changes, and the good fly angler is constantly tuned into those periods of transition. The gamefish you seek to tempt with flies will habitually and instinctively track the bait.

The following represent those baits most prevalent in the waters of the Northeast, mid-Atlantic, and Southeast that are of importance to fly fishermen.

Sand Eel (*Ammodytes americanus*)

Also known as sand lance, this baitfish is a primary source of food for most inshore species, and it is a important baitfish for fly anglers fishing the surf. In the waters of the Northeast, sand eels are often present in abundant numbers. Past seasons have seen large masses of sand eels close to shore during both the spring months and then again

Sand eel.   (Photo credit: Henry Cowen)

during the fall migratory run of gamefish. This phenomenon caused striped bass to migrate within the surf zone from New England to New Jersey, creating many fine surf and backwater opportunities for fly anglers.

Sand eels are slim in size, with an average mature length of four to six inches; specimens of seven to eight inches are not uncommon. In the spring of the year, much smaller, immature sand eels amass in large congregations; this is a time of plenty for the gamefish that prey upon them, especially striped bass.

Sand eel coloration varies from dark to light depending on the habitat they occupy, but they typically take on topside hues of olive, brown, blue-green, with a dirty-white underbelly, and silvery flanks. Often, a lavender or violet iridescent hue is noticeable along their sides.

Sand eels are most often found in sandy areas along beaches, shoals, and backwaters and typically in large, tightly packed schools. They frequent the extreme shallows as well as much deeper water. I have often been surrounded by literally hundreds, if not thousands, of swimming sand eels and the gamefish that feed on them. One of the characteristics that makes sand eels readily distinguishable from other baitfish is their undulating side-to-side swimming motion.

A significant behavior of sand eels is their routine of quickly burrowing into the sand, most notably along the fringes of the shoreline. The eels seem predisposed to doing this at high tide, in proximity to the low water locations. It is believed they burrow for purposes of seeking a resting place and safe haven while awaiting the next high tide and the arrival of dawn. Most of this burrowing activity takes place in the period around dusk, and predator species of fish seem especially keyed to this behavior. Knowing this gives the fly angler a decided advantage for two reasons. The first is that the eels tend to burrow in close inshore locations well within fly-rod casting range, and second, flies are, ideally, imitations that mimic the long slender shape of sand eels and their undulating swimming motions.

During periods of sand eel swarms, it is not at all uncommon for surf fly anglers to routinely out-fish spinning and conventional fishermen. When large numbers of sand eels are present in an area, a significant tactic is to seek them out, look for the eels, and understand their holding patterns and movements. If the eels frequent an area long enough, bass and other gamefish will become conditioned to those habits and key in on them. Diving terns are another indication that sand eels may be present. This is when the fly angling opportunity is at its best.

Any sparsely tied fly patterns that present a slender profile and match the coloration of the prevalent sand eels work well. It is advantageous to tie sand eel flies in a number of different color combinations to cover the spectrum of hues and tones that sand eels display. A beneficial tying approach is to blend some of those colors together; an especially productive blend for me has been olive, light tan, dark brown, white with just a hint of gold, and lavender. While I prefer natural material, I have found that synthetic body materials such as crystal flash and poly-braids also produce excellent results. When fishing sand eel flies, a slow retrieve with periodic erratic twitches is preferred. In currents, a dead drift through the area will produce results. Cast up current, mend the line, and allow the fly to sink. An occasional twitch of the line or rod tip helps simulate a wounded sand eel. During the evening hours, it may help to use a fly that is slightly weighed at the head, like a Clouser or Jiggy. Allow the fly to settle on the bottom, and then apply a short quick strip. This will cause the fly to kick up puffs of sand, replicating what takes place as a sand eel attempts to burrow. When fishing in this fashion the takes can be hard or quite subtle. Strip setting when the fly appears to have its motion halted often results in a hook-up.

Sand Eel Fly Sampler: AJ's Sand Eel (Forzano), RLS Small Eelie (Abrames), Sili Sand Eel (Steinberger), Soft Top Sand Eel (Starke), Sparkling Sand Eel (Windram), Epoxy Baitfish Sand Eel (Mikkleson), PJ Sand Eel (Peluso), Spring and Fall Lance (Haag), Surf Candy (Popovics), small slender Deceivers (Kreh), Clousers, Yak Hair Sand Eel, Angel Hair Sand Eel, Giant Sand Eel (Skok), Floating Sand Eel (Puglisi), Corsair Sand Eel (Gartside), BMAR Sand Eel (Marino), Ray's Fly (Bondorew), Enrico's Sand Eel (Puglisi).

Atlantic Silverside (*Menidia menidia*)

The Atlantic silverside is another principal baitfish that all East Coast gamefish forage upon. This baitfish is also referred to as spearing. Silversides are an abundant species and can vary in size from a couple of inches to larger specimens of six or seven inches. Most range from two to about five inches. This is another long,

Atlantic silverside.   (Photo credit: Justin Pellegrino)

slender-bodied baitfish with a somewhat fuller shape than the sand eel. Spearing have a green-gray coloration on top, with translucent transitioning to a white underbelly. They also have the appearance of dark brown flecking along the mid-portion of the flanks. Silversides have relatively small heads with prominently large eyes. The region around the head and nose areas appears as a shade of gray. Its flanks are highlighted by a silvery lateral line—hence their name—bordered by black striping.

Silversides are most often found in near-shore areas in shallow water with a sand or gravel bottom. You will find silversides along the shallow water off beaches. They also frequent back bays, harbors, inlets, and jetties, as well as sand and grass flats. Typically, spearing remain in the shallows for much of the year, venturing to deeper water in the winter months seeking their preferred temperature zone. They characteristically grow to a maximum length of about five or six inches, but on rare occasions larger specimens will be encountered, especially during the early fall months.

Schools of silversides tend to suspend in the water column and are frenetic swimmers when chased by gamefish. They dart and dash about and will leap from the surface of the water to escape pursuers. These behaviors lend themselves to a variety of fly retrieves when fishing in the presence of spearing. At times a dead drift, "do-nothing" retrieve is effective, letting the actions of the fly itself do all the work. When fishing in this fashion, periodically impart a slight twitching motion to the drifting fly as if it just made a flick of its tail. When silversides are being foraged upon by gamefish, a more erratic and faster retrieve outperforms slower retrieves. In situations where fast swimming fish like bonito, false albacore, or Spanish mackerel are on the feed, an overhand, double-stripping retrieve works best since it simulates a fast fleeing silverside. It pays to vary the retrieve in any given circumstance to discover which speed and style of retrieve stimulates the strike response.

Silverside Fly Sampler: Epoxy Baitfish (Mikkleson), Epoxy Spearing (Mikkleson), Deceiver (Kreh), Half and Half (Kreh/Clouser), Surf Candy (Popovics), Silverside Bunny, Secret Silverside (Gartside), Wounded Silverside (Marino), Silverside Muddler (Lindquist), Spearing Fly (Popovics), Deep Minnow (Clouser), Foxy Bone (Peluso), Silverside Bunny (Nault), Holographic Silverside (Veverka), Immature Spearing (Avondolio), Sili Spearing (Steinberger), Shimmer Fly (Sfakianos), Pretender Silverside (Starke), Rhody Flatwing (Abrames, Peabody, Thomas), Sandy's Silverside (Noyes), Perfect Minnow Olive, Puglisi Silver, EP Glass Minnow, Emerald Shiner (Puglisi).

Atlantic Menhaden (*Brevoortia tyrannus*)

The menhaden is more commonly referred to as mossbunker or simply bunker. This large, deep-bodied baitfish is a favored food of large striped bass and blue-

Menhaden.   (Photo credit: Chris Paparo)

fish and represents one of the most important fisheries along the entire length of the Atlantic coast, from Florida to Nova Scotia. Those specimens found in the Long Island area can grow to a length of about fifteen inches and attain a weight of approximately one pound. The largest and oldest specimens can reach a length of twenty inches and weigh as much as three pounds. Bunker are one of the largest baitfish classes of importance to the fly fisherman. Once very prolific, the menhaden population fell victim to overfishing and its stocks have since been managed collectively by the Atlantic States Marine Fisheries Commission Management Plan. As a result, bunker populations are now considered to be "healthy," but not yet back to peak levels of the 1950s and 1960s.

Menhaden have a deep-bodied profile. Their coloration includes metallic silvery flanks, a blue-green/blue-brown back, and a dark spot behind the gill area with several other spots along the flanks. Their bodies also convey a yellowish or brassy patina. Bunker are built with a prominent forked tail. They travel in large schools, usually very close to the surface of the water, so much so that when a school of bunker is present in an area, the angler will most often notice the tips of their tails and fins breaking the surface. When bunker take up residence in an area, especially a harbor or bay, it is not long before predatory species find them. At times you will find large bass and bluefish under the bunker, feeding at will. While this occurs most often in deeper water accessible by boat, bunker will move within range of the shore angler. I've experienced that happening off of rock and jetty formations inside harbors. This is a perfect time to use larger bunker patterns, preferably on a sinking line to get the fly down beneath the surface activity and to where the bass or blues lurk. If big bluefish are in the area under these conditions it is advisable to use a heavy shock leader or even tie-able wire, as the strikes will be vicious and frenzied. I prefer heavy fluorocarbon as a tippet, since it is less likely to cause big bass to become line shy. You may lose some bluefish but gain a nice bass. While a variety of retrieves can be used to fish big bunker flies, imparting a slow undulating motion seems to work best, since it isolates the fly as a somewhat injured and susceptible bait.

Bunker Fly Sampler: Acrylic Bunker (Mikkleson), Rainbow Bunker (McMurray), Bozo Bunker (Northrop), Tommy's Bunker (Thomas), Veil Fly Bunker (Lindquist), Bill's Bunker (Peabody), Bulky Bunker (Apfel/Smith), Dino's Bunker (Torino), Moriches Mouthful (Killen, Dunkerley), Big Deceivers (Kreh), RLS Crazy Menhaden, RLS Striper Moon (Abrames), Yak Attack (Scavette), Slammer Bunker (Sedotti), Adult Bunker (Puglisi).

Peanut Bunker (*Brevoortia tyrannus*)

This is the immature form of menhaden or bunker, and is especially relevant bait from late summer through the fall. Adult menhaden spawn from March through May and during September and October. By the time the fall migration of gamefish gets underway, these juvenile bunker or "peanuts" have grown to a size of about one and a half to seven inches. In proportions and coloration, peanut bunker are miniature replicas of their larger relatives. The small specimens tend toward a much more vivid silvery effect to their flanks. Most effective peanut flies include white, blue-green, black, lavender, and silver components. Every major gamefish in areas where peanuts are present forage on them and the blitzes can be quite dramatic. It is not uncommon during the fall run—when peanut bunker are heavily preyed upon by

Peanut bunker.

striped bass and bluefish—for massive numbers of the bait to fling themselves onto the beaches to escape their pursuers.

Peanut Bunker Fly Sampler: Peanut Butter (Puglisi), Blackwater Baby Bunker (Mitchell), MBAR Wounded Peanut (Marino), The Natural (Cowen), Crease Fly (Blados), Dino's Baby Bunker (Torino), Don's Peanut (Avondolio), Geno's Baby Angel (Quigley), Glimmer Bunker (Haag), Veil Peanut Bunker (Dunkerley), Pretender Baby Bunker (Starke), RK's Immature Bunker (Kress).

Bay Anchovy (*Anchoa mitchilli*)

Bay anchovies are small, slender fish that reach a maximum size of about three and a half inches in length. They are translucent with mostly silver and white hues. Bay anchovies have prominent dark eyes, a white/silvery belly sac and a silvery line running laterally along its flanks. Under certain light conditions you can also detect small traces of a lavender or pink tint in the body. Bay anchovies are found along the coast and in estuarine areas. They frequent shoals, reefs, jetties, harbors, inlets, flats, deep water, and areas close to beaches. Often referred to as rain bait, large schools of anchovies cause a dimpling effect on the water's surface. At times there are so many fish causing the surface disturbance, it appears as though it is raining. Anchovies travel in large schools and are vigorously pursued by gamefish. Bay anchovies are one of the most favored forage species of false albacore. In many instances, they key in specifically on the anchovies, and when this happens, the catch-ability runs the gamut from easy to almost impossible.

A number of retrieving techniques work well when fish are feeding on anchovies. A fast double overhand retrieve will often tempt tuna to strike out at a rapidly

Bay Anchovy.   (Photo credit: Ray Stachelek)

fleeing fly. Yet sometimes a dead drift with periodic twitches of the line will draw results. At other times long, steady pulls of line are the ticket. It pays to vary one's retrieve when bay anchovies are the targeted bait.

Bay Anchovy Fly Sampler: Royal Anchovy (Lindquist), Al-Bie Simple (Dixon), Monchovie (Dunkerley), Anchovy Bunny (Moekens), Rainfish (Haag), No-Bay-Vy (Haag), Marabou Candy (Lindquist), Joe's Small Fry (Scandore), Bay Anchovy, Epoxy Baitfish, (Mikkleson), Bonito Bunny (Boyle), Bonito Bear (Nault), Cyn-Chovy (Dapra), Brown Albie, Blue Albie (Brown), Easy Anchovy (Thompson), EP Anchovy (Puglisi), Golden Helmut (Becker), Hue Shifting Bay Anchovy (Eng).

American Eel (*Anguilla rostrata*)

It is well known that large American eels are among the best baits for trophy striped bass. Flies tied to imitate all stages of an eel's development are also quite effective tools for the fly angler. The phases of the eel's development that are of importance are: the glass-eel stage; the elvers; and the mature eels. Glass eels are transparent in color and about two and a half inches in length. They enter bays and estuaries in the fall and begin a process whereby their bodies become pigmented. As eels mature, they begin to develop a coloration that is green-brown to yellow brown on the top, with flanks that highlight silvery-bronze hues, and a gray-white to pure white underbelly. Eels are known to change their coloration in response to light and background and habitat color. They are snakelike in appearance, and can grow quite large. While male specimens achieve a length of about eighteen inches,

American eel. (Photo credit: Paul Peluso)

females can reach a length of four feet or more. The American eel is catadromous, spending most of its life in fresh water and migrating to salt water to spawn, most notably in the Sargasso Sea.

For all practical purposes, flies that range from several inches up to about twelve inches are the most sensible sizes for fly fishing. Considering that eels swim with a serpentine or snakelike motion, any flies used should attempt to replicate those characteristics. Natural materials like long saddle hackles, schlappen or rabbit strips, or large chenille produce a very nice action when fished in rips, currents, eddies, or other areas that attract and hold eels. Even in still water locations, those materials with slow and variable retrieves will produce results.

Eel Fly Sampler: All American Eel (Haag), Snake Fly (Tabory), Brown & Olive Snake (Schwack), Don's Elver Eel (Avondolio), Frank's Wooly Eel (Abbate), RLS Eel Punt, American Eel, (Abrames), South Shore Eel (Forzano), Midnight Rider (Peluso), Whiskey & Soda (Gustavson), EP Eel (Puglisi).

Hickory Shad (*Alosa mediocris*)

Hickory shad are of importance not only as a gamefish but also as a preferred bait of predatory fish like striped bass and bluefish. Shad often commingle with striped bass, especially in the spring, and will most often travel in pods or small schools. Depending upon the size of the bass, they either feed with or forage upon shad. There are usually large numbers of school-sized bass in and among the shad and they strike the same flies as shad. Often, this early season fishing is keyed in on the presence of small immature sand eels. In a classic food-chain scenario, shad and smaller bass feed on the sand eels and large bass feed on the shad. A big striper can consume even the largest of shad. I have had hickory shad up to about four pounds assaulted by large stripers, and watched as the bass swam around with the shad's tail protruding from their mouths; bass feed gluttonously on shad. Long, lean, and

Hickory shad.

hungry early season bluefish also prey on shad. While the bigger stripers ingest the shad whole, big bluefish frequently incapacitate the shad by first biting off the tail or simply chomping the shad down to size, then picking up the pieces.

Far and away, the best flies for replicating shad have been very large Deceivers, yak hair flies, and slimmed-down bunker patterns tied with both natural and synthetic materials. I tie one shad fly that is primarily an oversized half and half, which incorporates all of the tones and highlights of a shad. It is a blended pattern of saddle hackles, bucktail, and flash, utilizing colors of olive, dark green, yellow, white, black, lavender, chartreuse, and light blue. Under the right conditions of illumination, all these colors can be seen in a hickory shad. Additionally they are all colors that striped bass will respond to.

Shad Fly Sampler: Large Deceiver; Large Half and Half, EP Peacock (Puglisi), Yak Shad Fly, RLS Patterns (Abrames), Schlappen Deceiver, Slammer (Sedotti).

Finger Mullet (*Mugil cephalus*)

Also known as white, silver, or striped mullet, the "finger" connotation is used in reference to immature mullet. This baitfish can be observed jumping from the water and tail slapping as they careen across the surface. Of relevance to the fly angler this smaller member of the mullet clan averages between two and a half to six inches in length. Mullet have an extensive range—from New England to Florida. While difficult to distinguish in juvenile stages, the most mostly likely specimen to be encountered is the striped mullet and occasionally—if water temperatures are conducive—white mullet. Mullet can be found along sandy beaches, in harbors, in-

Finger mullet.   (Photo credit: Rich Santos)

lets, and estuaries. They can also be seen jumping and tail slapping on the inside elbows of jetties.

The mullet has a blue-gray upper body, with the flanks transitioning to silver hues—its sides also have black horizontal bars. The underbelly region is white. A few distinctive characteristics are a small mouth, blunt nose, and a second dorsal fin located behind the primary dorsal. These juvenile stage fish migrate inshore and range from about one inch in size to five inches—perfect fly-rod sizes. They frequent tidal creeks, harbors, bays, and other estuarine areas. Mullet are fast swimmers, often moving with erratic motions. Alternating steady retrieves with variable short pulls works well. When mullet flee pursuing predators, a faster retrieve can be employed.

Mullet Fly Sampler: EP Mullet, EP Finger Mullet (Puglisi), Soft-Top Mullet (Starke), Wooly Mullet (Haag), September Day Fly, September Night Fly (Abrames), Deceivers (Kreh).

American Butterfish (*Peprilus triacanthus*)

Butterfish are a coastal and offshore baitfish. While not as consistently significant to surf anglers as are some other baits, butterfish do deserve a mention. If they are encountered, a wide variety of standard fly patterns will successfully mimic the fish.

The coloration of butterfish is a gray blue on top with silvery pale flanks, a silver belly, and plentiful dark spots. The fish gets its name from its oily consistency and resultant slippery feel. Its body design is deep and thin, somewhat like pompa-

Butterfish.   (Photo credit: Ray Stachelek)

no. Some of the more prominent features of butterfish are the rounded, squat head, and small mouth, and distinctively pointed pectoral fins. Most often encountered on the east end of Long island, butterfish move about in small schools that tend to remain near the surface. They also frequent bays, harbors, and other inshore coastal areas. Butterfish in the six- to nine-inch range are of most relevance to the fly angler.

Butterfish Fly Sampler: There aren't many specific local butterfish patterns available but you can use mullet, peanut bunker, herring, or generic deeper-bodies flies and adjust the coloration. Long Island fly tier Enrico Puglisi has a number of fly pattern designs that can be modified to create good butterfish imitations; BMAR Wounded Butterfish (Marino).

Atlantic Mackerel (*Scomber scombrus*)

Long considered a favorite live or cut bait for large striped bass, the presence of Atlantic mackerel can signal an opportunity for the fly fisherman, especially the smaller "tinker" class. Mackerel are sleek, strong swimmers and sport very attractive coloration and marking. Their topside conveys iridescent blue-green tones, with silver-white flanks and underbelly. Numerous black bars adorn the upper portion of the mackerel's body. The largest specimens can attain a weight of about two pounds, but the average weights are a pound or less. If they do appear in local waters, mackerel first show in the late spring, both inshore and offshore. Juvenile mackerel can be present well into the fall months. While not as abundant as during the 1960s, mackerel stocks have been slowly rebounding.

Immature tinker mackerel frequent estuaries, harbors, and bays. The appearance of specimens that range from about three to six inches are important to fly fishing. The largest of this mackerel species can grow in excess of twenty inches and

Atlantic mackerel.   (Photo caption: Paul Peluso)

weigh more than two pounds. Like shad, large mackerel are also a great fish to catch on the fly rod; small, bright flies work very well.

Mackerel Fly Sampler: One of the best all-time mackerel flies is Bill Catherwood's Tinker Mackerel. It set the standard for all mackerel flies that would follow; big Deceivers, Yak Mac (Scavette), Sedotti Mackerel, EP Mackerel, EP Tinker Mackerel (Puglisi), RLS Tinker Mac, RLS Tinker's Green (Abrames), Flat Wing Tinker Mackerel (Eng), The Holy Mackerel (Faulkingham).

Shrimp

All gamefish love shrimp, probably even more than humans do. In certain regions of the East Coast, some fishermen won't even think about heading out to the water without a bucket of shrimp as bait. While pink, white, or brown shrimp provide a substantial food source for many gamefish along the east coast, a smaller variety of shrimp is of importance to inshore fly fishing: it is the smaller grass, or common, shrimp. It can be found in tidal creeks, estuaries, salt marshes on the incoming tide, and drifting upon the currents during outgoing tidal movements. Typically grass shrimp are found in shallow water. These shrimp are small, between one and two two inches in length and have a very transparent appearance. They primarily inhabit shoreline cover and take up sheltered residence in the grass within salt ponds and marsh areas. They move in and out of these areas with the tides and, as such, become vulnerable to predators.

The sand shrimp is another common variety. It too frequents estuaries and other similar habitat preferred by grass shrimp. Their body shape is flat with a transparent look to it. Their coloration is subtly grayish with brown or black markings. Their color and markings act as camouflage against the sand. They are a burrowing

Shrimp.

shrimp that remain in the sand during the day and move out at night to feed. Sand shrimp grow to a length of about three inches.

Shrimp Fly Sampler: Bottom Shrimp (Lindquist), EP Grass Shrimp, Spawning Shrimp, Suspended Shrimp, Flex Squid (Puglisi), Floating Grass Shrimp (Robl), Foam-back Shrimp (Mikkleson), Mini-Me (Dixon), Pink Lady (Caolo), Simple Shrimp (Avondolio), Ultra Shrimp (Popovics), Golden Swimming Shrimp (Patlen).

Northern Shortfin Squid (*Illex illecebrosus*) and Inshore Longfin Squid (*Loligo pallida*)

The squid species most relevant to fly fishing are the northern shortfin squid and the inshore longfin squid, with the former having a greater presence inshore. Most of these squid are smaller than twelve inches in length but the longfin can reach a length of twenty-four inches. Squid are cephalopods and are close relatives of the octopus, cuttlefish, and nautilus. A unique trait of squid is that they quickly change size and shape when a need arises for camouflage. They are also capable of emitting a stream of dark ink when threatened and attempting to escape. Squid propel themselves with an internal jet propulsion system, which means they can move quite fast—faster than we are capable of stripping a fly line! But squid also remain suspended in water, so a varied retrieve works well. Squid can also change colors to match the surrounding environment or when stressed. Their skin is basically translucent and can have highlighted iridescent tones of pink or lavender, red, purple, brown, white, yellow, green, and black and can mix and match colors to blend into their surroundings.

Squid. (Photo credit: Chris Paparo)

The combination of striped bass, small squid, and rips can work to create some of the most memorable of flyfishing days. When keyed in on squid, gamefish feed aggressively and voraciously.

Squid Fly Sampler: Offshore Epoxy Squid (Mikkleson), Almost Calamari (Marino), AJ's Epoxy Squid (Forzano), Body Fur Squid (Dunkerley), Electric Squid (Lindquist), Harvey's Squid (Cooper), Squid Crease Fly (Blados/Mikkleson), Bailey's Squid (Fleischmann), RLS Squid Flies (Abrames), Fireball Squid (Cordeiro), Magic Squid (Caolo), Flex Squid (Puglisi).

Crabs

Most all prized inshore gamefish forage on crabs. There are a number of crab species of importance to the East Coast fly angler: fiddler crab, blue crab, green crab, mud and calico crabs, and the ever growing population of invasive Asian crabs. While most inshore gamefish forage on crabs, striped bass are particularly fond of them. Of importance to the fly angler are the size, shape, coloration, and movements of crabs. Color varies by species. As the names imply, blue and green crabs display overtones of those respective colors. The smaller crabs tend to be the most relevant to fly fishing. Larger growing large crabs like the blue claw are important during their juvenile stages. At times crabs move about the bottom, float in midwater column ranges, and during "hatches" can be seen very close to the surface. During new moon tides of the spring and summer, immature crabs can be spotted drifting immediately below the surface of the water. This occurs as they move out from estuaries, back bays, harbors, and salt ponds.

Crabs.

Crab flies are most often fished on sand or mud flats or the shallow fringes of beaches where rocks are present. This is a slow, deliberate technique usually involving sight fishing. Under these situations, a stealthy approach and accurate delivery of the fly are the critical keys to success. When small crabs float on the currents, a fly can be drifted along with them, either with a total dead drift or with a subtle swimming action imparted to the fly.

Generic Crab Sampler: Del's Merkin (Brown), Crab-a-Dab-Goo (Mikkleson), Palmetto Rattling Crab, EP Crag, EP Fuzzy Crab (Puglisi), Green Diablo (Caolo), BMAR Crab (Marino), Mark's Juvee Crab (Gustavson), Stone Crab (Samson), Don's Crab (Avondolio), Live Body Defense Crab (Murphy).

Clam Worm (*Alitta succinea*)

When fly anglers reference a worm "hatch," it is the clam or cinder worm that is the object of discussion. Basically, a clam worm is a sandworm. The hatch is actually a spawning swarm that typically occurs with the full and new moon tides during both spring and early summer months. Most anglers who regularly fish the swarms do so at night and prefer calm, hot conditions with little or no wind. Yet, similar activity can occur during the very early to midmorning hours. The spawning activity takes place in back bays, calm sections of harbors, estuaries, and even along quiet open beaches and shoals. The clam worm's coloration is primarily an opalescent reddish brown but can show traces of green and copper. It can grow to a maximum length of six to eight inches, yet the "hatch" specimens are but a few inches in length. The worm has a distinct head region and a segmented body.

Clam worm. (Photo credit: Justin Pellegrino)

Clam Worm Fly Sampler: Devil Worm (Dixon), Cinderworm (Robl), Cinderworm (Windram).

American Lobster (*Homarus americanus*)

Gamefish will often forage on juvenile lobster if they are available regionally. Recreational fishermen who regularly fish Northeast waters often find partially digested lobsters in the stomachs of harvested striped bass. For purposes of fly fishing, the smaller lobsters are of importance. Flies in the four- to six-inch range

Lobster.

work quite well. A number of successful patterns use color blends of red, black, orange, and green.

Lobster Fly Samplers: Crayfish patterns can work especially well to replicate small lobsters. EP Fibers Crayfish by Enrico Puglisi are especially effective and can be tied in a wide range of colors and sizes to match the juvenile lobster.

Herring (*Clupea harengus*) and Alewives (*Alosa pseudoharengus*)

Atlantic, blueback, and threadfin herring are all of local importance to the fly angler. Most anglers eagerly anticipate the seasonal arrival of these baits, for it is a leading food source for big gamefish. This is the time of year that fly anglers have some of the best chances to catch big bass on the fly. When herring amass in large migrating schools and the first of the gannets are seen foraging on them, large striped bass are not far behind. Blueback herring and alewife are also known as river herring. Atlantic herring inhabit coastal areas and waters of the continental shelf. Juvenile herring, often referred to as "sardines" are found in large schools in shallower water during the summer months. These immature herring are about one and one-half inches in length. Adult herring can attain a weight of one and a half pounds and have a deep thin body, with a pointed nose and large mouth. They also are equipped with a tail that is deeply forked. Their coloration runs from a green-blue back with silvery flanks and underbelly. Threadfin herring and flies that imitate them are eaten by tarpon, snook, redfish, and jacks.

Alewives are closely related to herring and are also an anadromous species, migrating to fresh water to spawn. Immature alewives remain in freshwater rivers

Herring.   (Photo credit: Paul Peluso)

from spring until the fall when they migrate to salt water as water temperatures become cooler.

The alewife has silvery flanks with blue-green hues and bronze overtones on the topside region, and a whitish underbelly. They are a deep-bodied fish with a prominently large eye. Of most relevance to the fly fisherman are specimens six inches and under. They travel in thick schools and are an important forage species for many gamefish.

Herring/Alewife Fly Sampler: Big Deceivers (Kreh), Half and Half (Kreh/ Clouser), Acrylic Baitfish (Mikkleson), Blueback Herring (Puglisi), Magnum Baitfish Herring (Cowen), Glimmer Herring (Haag), BMAR Blue Herring (Marino), Veil Blueback Herring (Dunkerley), November Olive Herring (Eng), Slammer Blueback Herring (Sedotti).

Pilchards

Pilchards are classified generically as a type of sardine and are related to herring. Within the broad categories of sardines and pilchards, there are about twenty species of sardines and about a half dozen pilchard species. Within the context of the geography this book covers, pilchards are defined as small, sardine-like fish up to a length of about six inches. Pilchards are a prime baitfish often used by Southeast anglers to catch snook and redfish and as live chum when tossed about to attract

Pilchards/sardines.

gamefish or to stimulate a feeding bite. In the Southeast, pilchards are also categorized colloquially as whitebait. Deceivers, Deceiver variations, Half and Half flies, and baitfish fish flies, like those of Enrico Puglisi, work well as pilchard and sardine imitations.

Minnows and Other Small Baitfish

Minnows generally encompass a broad spectrum of small baitfish and the category includes mud minnows, marsh minnows, killies, chubs, mummichogs, and cacahoes. Most of these baitfish can be found in shallow inshore areas such as estuaries, around grass flats, sod banks, and other areas close in to the shoreline. Minnows will typically school up for protection or cruise about the shallows in small groupings. Regardless of their numbers they are regularly foraged upon by all shallow water

Minnow/mummichog.   (Photo credit: Chris Paparo)

Striped killfish. (Photo credit: Chris Paparo)

gamefish. Due to their size and shape diversity, minnows can be replicated by a wide variety of flies from simple to sublime.

Pinfish (*Lagodon rhomboides*)

Pinfish are a favored forage species of most inshore gamefish that are targets of the surf fly angler; snook, tarpon, redfish, and spotted trout will all feed on pinfish. This

Pinfish. (Photo credit: Pat Ford)

member of the porgy family frequents shallow water areas throughout much of the year, from early spring to the late fall when they locate along the surf zone, around sod banks and grass beds, and near-inshore structure like piers, docks, bridges, jetties, and reefs. Four- to six-inch flies replicate the most common size range for pinfish.

Spot (*Leiostomus xanthurus*)

This member of the croaker family is a baitfish similar in stature to pinfish. Spot inhabit inshore coastal waters throughout a significant portion of the East Coast and the Gulf of Mexico. It is prevalent in surf areas, estuaries, and back bays. Spot are a popular baitfish often fished live, and are easily recognized by a trademark black spot behind each gill plate. While its range technically extends from Maine to Florida, the greatest number of spot can be found from the mid-Atlantic region down through South Carolina. Predatory gamefish within that range will feed vig-

Spot. (Photo credit: Chris Paparo)

orously on spot. Fly patterns similar to those used for pinfish with suffice for both juvenile and adult spot.

Miscellaneous Baits

Most gamefish are innately opportunistic and, perhaps at times, even indiscriminate feeders. Most predatory gamefish will consume just about anything they can fit into their mouths. In addition to the primary baits previously listed, a number of other noteworthy forage deserve mention and can be replicated by a wide variety of fly patterns. Among those other incidental species are the juvenile stages of flounder, bluefish (snappers), small bergalls, blackfish, weakfish, porgies, sea robins, and needlefish.

Miscellaneous Fly Sampler: Flounder Clouser (Mikkleson), Flounder After a Bad Night (Sedotti), Bergall Deepster (Thompson), Needlefish (Veverka), Sea Robin (Dunkerley), Needlefish (Puglisi), Glimmer Pinfish, Wool Mummichog (Haag).

Chapter Nine

Essential Surf Fly Wallet

The fly angler had a dream that he was standing at The Gate awaiting his turn to meet Saint Peter, one of the greatest fishermen of all recorded time. While the fisherman was happy to have taken the "*up*" elevator, he knew all too well that he was going to be in big trouble. The keeper of the gate was never going to allow him to bring all his flies beyond the Pearly Gates. This angler had boxes upon boxes of favorite fly patterns. After all, who knew what heaven might mean to a fly fisherman, and what species of fish one would encounter in paradise. This fellow needed to be prepared. What fly fisher could blame him? As a fisherman, Saint Peter understood the fly angler's plight but he just shook his head and said, "My son, I will let you in but I must only allow you one small fly wallet. We already have too many fly fisherman up here with fur and feather creations, so a handful of flies will have to do." The angler was horrified and at that point awoke screaming from the nightmare. After wiping the sweat from his brow and calming down he thought about the implications of his Saint Peter encounter: If you could fish only "a handful" of flies for the rest of your life in the saltwater surf, what would they be?

I've often wondered about that too, and that if my life depended on catching a saltwater fish on a fly, what patterns I would I choose to tie onto my leader. What go-to flies might guarantee perpetual surf-fishing success? That's a tough question. The wide world of saltwater fly fishing is rife with a surplus of productive fly patterns. That abundance provides anglers with an almost infinite number of design possibilities since all flies have inherent potential for variation and modification. Over the course of researching and writing two fly pattern books, I've had the good fortune to talk with literally hundreds of flyfishing guides, captains, and professional or amateur fly tiers from Maine to the Texas Gulf Coast. I've gotten to interview some of the best flyfishing and fly-tying talent this great country has to offer. I've also had the unique opportunity to examine more than twelve hundred flies, including many of the best saltwater flies that have ever been tossed at fish. Some of those patterns were original designs but most were innovative modifications of tried and true designs, each in its own way a marvelous creation of art imitating life.

The highlight of those experiences was a note I received from the venerable Bernard Lefty Kreh, offering some kind words on my book, *Saltwater Flies of the Northeast*. His note gave me an excuse to call him to extend my thanks for the gracious comments. We had a wonderful chat and I mentioned to Mr. Kreh that one of the things I would want included as part of the fishing gear I take with me to the fly-fishing "hereafter" is an adequate supply of Lefty's Deceivers. I couldn't depend solely on Angel Hair patterns. I told Mr. Kreh I couldn't imagine entering heaven without his creation, so much so that I instructed my wife as to which Deceivers needed to be packed along with me. To be caught in a heavenly situation surrounded by all great fish without the right fly might just be a fly fisherman's purgatory . . . or worse.

But even in heaven, as in the surf, one fly is not practical, since all fish have different feeding preferences under varied conditions. Yet this limiting task could be daunting when selecting those flies that are considered indispensable. After much consideration, I decided upon a core of proven patterns as part of an essential surf fly wallet that would perform well form Maine to Florida. Some of these flies are specific patterns, while others could be classified as styles of tying that offer the angler or fly tier a platform from which suitable modifications or variations can be crafted. While certainly not all inclusive, the following proven designs will consistently get results.

Lefty's Deceiver

My first choice is an obvious and easy one. The Lefty's Deceiver is the epitome of a fly pattern. When pressed to choose but one fly to count on in a pinch, many

An original Lefty's Deceiver tied by Bernard "Lefty" Kreh.

saltwater fly anglers across the globe reach for the respected Lefty's Deceiver or some fitting variation. No matter where I have fished, I've seen Deceivers of some size, shape, or form in fly boxes, even on remote tidal streams on the Alaska Peninsula. The fly is time-tested and remarkably effective. As a pattern, the original and its countless variations have most likely accounted for more fish than any other fly design in the era of modern fly fishing. It is hailed as one of the greatest patterns of all time. It is also one of the most imitated patterns in all of fly fishing. I once counted more than a hundred variations of Deceivers offered for sale in various catalogs and online websites. Even within the realm of flies, imitation is the truest form of flattery.

Most anglers who regularly fish the Deceiver have tweaked it a bit to suit personal preferences and needs, and that is the true beauty of the fly: it lends itself to tinkering. In Lefty's words, the Deceiver is a "style of pattern," rather than a single fly. The implication is that a tier can add a personal mark to a very versatile and adaptable pattern. Just about every fish that swims loves this fly in some form or another. In the course of my own fly fishing with the Deceiver, I have caught striped bass, bluefish, Atlantic bonito, little tunny, Spanish mackerel, northern weakfish, seatrout, snook, jacks, redfish, tarpon, Pacific salmon, largemouth and smallmouth bass, and a large cast of other gamefish in fresh water and salt water. In its infinite variations, the fly can replicate most any baitfish size and coloration. By varying the fly-tying materials, one can also change the profile of the fly to more closely replicate the silhouette of most prey species. Depth management for fishing the layers of the water column can be effectively achieved through the use of appropriately matched lines: floating, intermediate sink tips, high-density sink tips, and full sinking lines.

Clouser Deep Minnow

Hot on the heels of the Deceiver as an essential wallet choice is Bob Clouser's original Deep Minnow. Clouser created his world-famous "minnow" for smallmouth bass in his home water, the Susquehanna River. The pattern's reputation grew

An original Clouser Deep Minnow tied by Bob Clouser.

exponentially as its success grew, measured not only in terms of numbers of fish caught but also in the diversity of species succumbing to its effective design. Like the Deceiver, the Clouser has taken most fish it has been cast to, both in fresh water and salt water. In many respects—and as is the case with most all truly great flies—there is simplicity in its design. Fundamentally, the fly is an upside-down hair pattern with a wing, some flash, and a pair of barbell eyes set like those of a predecessor, the Crazy Charlie, or some earlier flies of anonymous origins in the Southeast and Gulf Coast regions of the United States. As one Gulf Coast fly angler told me, "The first thing we did when Wapsi created dumbbell eyes was tie them on to make flies sink deeper."

But the genius of the Deep Minnow is in the way the components are assembled. It is one of those flies that makes you say, "Now why didn't I think of that?" As with some famous entertainers, this fly has become known by just one name: "Clouser." It is a very versatile fly, adaptable to size, color, and profile preferences. While there is actually one original and specific tying recipe for the fly, it has proven successful in many modified forms. The fly can be tied in slender profile or in micro-to-magnum sizes, and the basic design can be modified for use with any number of natural or synthetic tying materials. Weight management can also be achieved through the use of varying size barbell eyes.

Half and Half

One cannot reference the Deceiver and the Clouser without at least a mention of their progeny, the Half and Half. When one considers the enormous success of both parent patterns, it only stands to reason that a hybrid of the two flies would double your productivity. The fly gets its name because it is tied half as a Deceiver

The hybrid half and half tied by Paul Schwack, Jr.

and half as a Clouser, utilizing the best attributes of each pattern. Interestingly, it was both Kreh and Clouser who first fused their original flies into the crossbreed design. Like its parent flies, the Half and Half is so effective, it too has spawned an entire class of flies patterned from its design. While a purely impressionistic fly, the hybrid leaves plenty of room for creative tinkering to suit various fishing conditions. Personally, I like to tie mine heavily weighted—with oversized dumbbell eyes—so that it can be used as a dredging pattern when fish lay deep in currents or simply near the bottom in a neutral feeding mood. Tied in larger sizes this is a productive big fish fly.

Epoxy Baitfish

The generic epoxy baitfish has earned a place of distinction among the best of the all-time fly patterns. It is a very versatile design and when tied properly it is well balanced, foul resistant, and extremely durable. The fly can also handle toothy critters like bluefish and Spanish mackerel. Epoxy baitfish patterns are representative of a tying style that utilizes various epoxies to form the main body or head area of a fly. One of the best epoxy fly designs are those tied by Glen Mikkleson. He has made tying epoxy flies an art form, and he has pioneered innovative techniques with both epoxy and acrylics. There are plenty of imitations of this fly on the market but few come close to the effectiveness of Mikkleson's original.

Expoxy baitfish flies tied by Glenn Mikkleson.

Epoxy flies suggest small to medium baitfish such as sand eels, silversides, bay anchovies, and numerous forms of white baits and minnows. In surf, a red and black version is very productive once the sun goes down. The generic epoxy baitfish pattern can be tied in numerous color combinations and is a productive fly for most coastal gamefish species. In the Northeast, the fly is a proven favorite for striped bass, bluefish, bonito, false albacore, skipjack, and small bluefin tuna. In the Southeast and Gulf Coast regions, snook, redfish, jacks, and trout readily eat the fly, as do all species of small tunas and mackerel. The fly has also been embraced by fly anglers on the west coast for their array of inshore species.

The Crease Fly

The world-renowned Crease Fly is the creative genius of Captain Joe Blados. While all tiers strive to produce flies that are new and different, in reality, very few ever accomplish that goal. Most new flies are typically design adaptations that represent variations of existing and proven patterns. But every once in a long while we witness true innovation in the art of fly tying—a fly design or technique that is so unique it changes the way we fish, and fundamentally changes the sport. One such innovative design technique led Joe Blados to create the Crease Fly, a pattern crafted to mimic the profile of the prolific immature bunker or menhaden. While originally conceived for the inshore fishery of the North Fork of Long Island, this fly has an established global track record of success and has devotees wherever it is has been fished. It has been embraced globally, and it has become a staple in the fly box of anglers pursuing gamefish that feed in the upper levels of the water column. I have

Crease Fly by Joe Blados, tied by Glenn Mikkleson.

witnessed the range of the Crease Fly's effectiveness from silver salmon in Alaska to the surface-feeding gamefish of the Yucatan Peninsula and all stops in between, in salt water and fresh. In magnum sizes, it is also a very effective offshore pattern for tuna and other large gamefish. What makes the Crease Fly a solid choice for the surf is its unique versatility? While built primarily for top-water fly fishing, Crease flies can be fished under the surface, fast, slow, and any speed in between; its action simply drives fish crazy. The Crease Fly can be tied in petite sizes for wary albies or as a jumbo fly for larger species.

Classic Hairwing

The hairwing class of patterns is one of the simplest of all fly designs and was one of the first to emerge during the 1950s, when saltwater fly fishing began to take hold in the Unites States. Those first flies used in the brine were adaptations of streamer flies used in fresh water. Over time the flies evolved to meet the demands of saltwater gamefish. One of the foremost classic hair wing patterns of the time was the Joe Brook's Blonde, a streamer fly. The Blonde has withstood the test of time and has been the structural basis upon which many other hair flies have been crafted. It is a classic saltwater fly pattern . . . a style of fly I used to fool my first striped bass. While the original tie has accounted for many varied species of freshwater and saltwater fish, the pattern lends itself well to numerous variations and enhancements. Tied simply, the fly sports a tail and a wing of bucktail combined with a body of silver tinsel. The head is typically built with black thread. It can be tied in most any color combination and size. The original versions were tied as the Platinum Blonde, Honey

Classic Hairwing tied by A. J. Forzano.

Blonde, Black Blonde, Strawberry Blonde, and Argentine Blonde. Over the years the tie has transformed into many other functional forms, including multi-wing hi-ties and wide profile synthetic hair flies, an example of which is Puglisi's Black and Purple Tarpon Fly. Through mixing and matching of hair colors, natural and synthetic tying materials, and tying methods, this class of flies can replicate many different bait forms that move in the surf and other shallow and inshore areas.

Crab, Creature, and Critter Flies

Crabs, crayfish, small lobsters, and shrimp are as much a dietary preference of desirable gamefish as they are a delight to the human palate. While there are many anatomically correct flies that replicate specific arthropods—and I would enjoy including on this list one fly replica of each—I do have to remind myself that the limit for the fly wallet is but a handful of pattern styles. So this fly selection is made for what I have come to refer to as a hybrid creature fly, a pattern style that blends the best attributes of each crustacean creature. One characteristic of creature flies is a very buggy-looking appearance and lots of inherent movement. Gamefish will eat crustacean flies drifted in currents and rips off deep water or on skinny water flats as they cruise about for the next meal. Striped bass on the flats love creature flies. As an impressionistic pattern that creates the illusion of an arthropod life form, the creature fly will often draw many fish to strike. Size and color variations to match

Crustacean Creature Fly tied by Angelo Peluso.

the prevalent crustaceans and bottom conditions are helpful under diverse fishing conditions.

For example, when fishing areas where crabs are present, it always pays to carry at least a light and a dark version of the pattern to match the bottom conditions and the carapace coloration. Bonefish, redfish, permit, and striped bass are especially partial to creature flies. Some other excellent examples of this design are: Caolo's Green Diablo and Pink Lady, Borski's Chernobyl Crab, and Curcione's Beach Bug.

Flatwing

The origins of this fabulous fly are attributed in part to the coloration of Ray's Fly and the flatwing tying concepts of New England's Ken Abrames and Bill Peabody. The combination of those two features resulted in a fly that can replicate an array of baitfish and be tied in any number of productive sizes. The fly fishes and casts exceptionally well and the flatwing hackle design adds an illusion of body mass when viewed from a fish's upward-looking perspective. The fly is a favorite among striped bass anglers and it is a wonderful pattern to experiment with, varying size and color to match prevalent baitfish. It imitates moderate to large baitfish as well as eels. This is also a great pattern to swing in currents using grease line mending techniques. The fly has a significant amount of intrinsic movement, making its design very appealing to many species of gamefish that frequent the surf.

Rhody Flatwing tied by Eric Peterson.

Ray's Fly

Perfection through simplicity of design is the best way to describe Ray's Fly, a creation of Ray Bondorew. This New England classic is an extremely versatile and effective pattern, ideal for replicating a wide assortment of small to midsized baitfish. The fly's origins extend back to the rocky shoreline of Narragansett, Rhode Island. The primary driver behind the fly's design was a desire to match the olive, yellow, pearl, and dark back coloration of the Atlantic silverside. Ray's Fly is one of the most effective Atlantic silverside (spearing) patterns of all time. I am often surprised that even some seasoned fly anglers are not familiar with this Rhody phenomenon. This fly is a must! When dressed sparsely, it performs exceptionally well as a sand eel imitation. If I have room in my fly wallet, I might also sneak in another of Bondorew's flies: the Bondorew Bucktail. This outstanding performer is often used in tandem with Ray's Fly, making for a very efficient combination.

Ray's Fly (bottom) and Bondorew Streamer (top) tied by Ray Bondorew.

Seaducer tied by A. J. Forzano.

Seaducer

This is one of my all-time favorite fly patterns and has fished well from the Northeast to the Southeast. It is the creation of Homer Rhode and was introduced in the 1940s as the Streamer Fly, a pattern designed for snook. It later became known as the Seaducer and has been used for many types of saltwater and freshwater game-fish. It is a very effective striped bass fly, especially when tied in red and white and fished in rips where squid are present. I've had some of my best striped bass fishing using this pattern in the Watch Hill rips when calamari are in abundance. I refer to the fly as being delicate and deadly, since it can be presented to wary fish like snook, yet it has a seductive appeal that drives most other fish crazy. When fishing deep, I like to add a set of barbell eyes that give an already enticing action some additional jigging motions. In addition to the red and white version, I like tying the Seaducer in blended yellow, green, and chartreuse. An all-black tie is a terrific nighttime fly. Alaska's salmon and rainbow also seem to like it when tied smaller and in suitable color combinations.

Marabou and Bunny Flies

Two of the most effective classes of flies that I have fished anywhere I've traveled are those that utilize marabou feathers or rabbit fur as the primary materials. Any crossbreed patterns that blend the best features of marabou and bunny—two tantalizing and seductive fly-tying materials—are effective. My arsenal of such patterns is sated with an array of flies tied with many size and color combinations. I

Marabou Bunny Fly tied by Angelo Peluso.

would not set foot in a tidal coho stream without a sampling of each style of fly and at least several such patterns in multiple colors. The effectiveness of a marabou and bunny combo pattern is legendary. In my own experiences the range of gamefish taken on that style of fly runs the gamut from bonefish, redfish, snook, and tarpon, to striped bass, seatrout, weakfish, bonito, Spanish mackerel, and small tunas, as well as numerous other saltwater and freshwater fish. In Alaska, size and color variations of the pattern have been deadly on all five species of salmon as well as trout, dollies, char, pike, and even grayling. Within the flyfishing community, this combo pattern seems to just have developed naturally without any one single tier credited with the creation. For avid fly anglers and tiers, it really doesn't take too much of a leap of faith to marry bunny and marabou. They are perfect together, and the fly is fun to fish.

Snake Fly

The heavenly fly or surf angler needs at least one eel-like pattern in his or her arsenal. None is better suited to that task than Lou Tabory's Snake Fly. The pattern

Tabory Snake Fly tied by Lou Tabory.

was developed in the late 1970s to simulate the Leiser Angus Fly. The effectiveness of the fly is attributed to its buoyancy, action, and adaptability. By varying the amount of materials used, the fly can be tied slim to medium to full-bodied, to match the profile of the available bait. It can be fished on a floating or sinking line. The more effective colors are black, white chartreuse, olive, or an assortment of blended colors. This is a great fly for big fish seeking a big meal and it works equally well fished seductively on the surface for bright silver salmon and pike. If you happen to get detoured "downstairs," it should work well with the sea serpents!

Jiggy

Very few lures are as consistently effective as a bucktail jig. The Jiggy was created by world-renowned fly angler and fly tier Bob Popovics as a fly version of a small jig. The Jiggy is another of those pattern styles that is often modified and varied for no other reason than it reliably catches fish. It is another example of a simple yet durable and effective tie. The weighted head of the Jiggy enables it to be fished in the lower portions of the water column and, depending on depth, close to or right on the

Jiggy tied by Bob Popovics.

bottom. Pauses in strips allow the fly to flutter and move like a jig. The fly presents a slim profile and it can be tied in a range of bait sizes and colors. Bounced along the bottom, few fish can resist the temptation to strike the Jiggy. Shallow-water fluke love the fly when fished with a full, high-grain sinking line.

So there you have it, my big handful of essential flies. I am certainly you will try many more but these are great go-to flies that will produce consistent results, here on earth or *up* there fishing with Saint Peter!

Chapter Ten

Beach Hat Tricks, Slams, and Long Shots

There is nothing coveted more in the world of fly fishing than catching multiple premier gamefish on the fly, and all in one day. Throughout Florida and other Southeast and Gulf Coast locales, the highest inshore fly angling honor belongs to those who catch a tarpon, a bonefish, and a permit on a fly during a single outing. Other similar accomplishments qualify for the recognition and involve species like redfish, snook, and spotted seatrout. The Northeast and mid-Atlantic regions of the East Coast have their own version of that prize, which includes striped bass, bluefish, little tunny, and Atlantic bonito. While most of this game plays out from the casting platform of a boat, there are fly anglers who also make the contest more interesting by wading after their quarry. The challenge is exponentially more difficult when undertaken on foot.

Although nomenclature may vary regionally for describing these accomplishments, they can be classified into three categories: hat tricks, slams, and grand slams. And there is even a super version of the slam. There are some places like Mexico's Yucatan Peninsula where the probability for success is greater than elsewhere for the highly coveted tarpon, bonefish, and permit slam, yet even in Ascension Bay the task can be daunting. I've also pursued slams wading Alaska waters for all five species of Pacific salmon. In the Northeast and mid-Atlantic regions, anglers have their own opportunity for a grand slam. This unique "home run" of fly fishing involves catching a striped bass, bluefish, false albacore, and bonito all in the same day and all on a fly. A weakfish also qualifies as a species that can be substituted in the slam. The IGFA refers to this milestone as an Inshore Super Grand Slam and now awards a special certificate to those fortunate enough to have accomplished this goal.

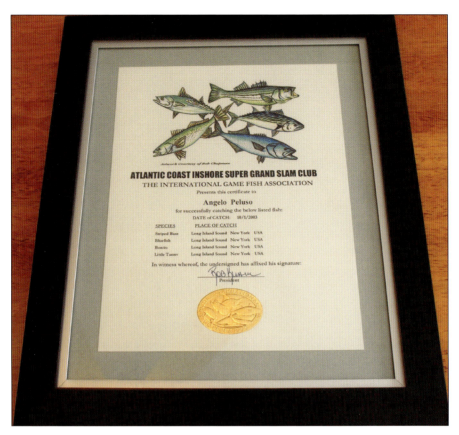

Plaque from the Atlantic Coast Inshore Super Grand Slam Club.

Consistently achieving the slam from the surf is very rewarding, and something one specifically sets out to do. To be successful the angler needs to maintain a very positive, "can-do" mindset. While it can, and sometimes does, just happen by chance, this is not generally the kind of fishing activity that lends itself to serendipity. Therefore, the wading fly-fisherman should have a strategy and a plan if a slam is the objective of a day's outing. As you will see, it also helps having a modicum of discipline and focus.

Defining Terms

According to the encyclopedia, a hat trick is an occurrence in sports, ". . . associated with succeeding at anything three times in three consecutive attempts." While this accomplishment has roots in the English game of cricket, it has been given its most visible meaning in the United States in the game of ice hockey, where it refers to one player scoring three goals in a single game. What's good for ice hockey is good for fishing, and it didn't take long for some in the flyrodding crowd to anoint the hat trick or slam designation upon those who successfully land three premier species of fish on the fly in any one day. Taking this achievement a step further, and up a notch, any four species caught on a fly in a single day is referred to as a grand slam in honor of that magnificent achievement that is part of our national pastime. A number of Northeast fly anglers are fortunate each year to manage a hat trick or a grand slam, and a select few have been recognized by the IGFA for such an accomplishment. For many anglers, the hat trick or the slam is a function of chance—being in the right place at the right time. But for others it is the result of a planned and disciplined execution. There is no better time to achieve this flyfishing objective in the Northeast than during the months from August to October, with October being the peak month. Those who fish the mid-Atlantic can extend that peak into November and, weather permitting, the early days of December. Fly anglers who wade about the waters of the Southeast have a much wider window of opportunity the farther south they go, and can enjoy success at this game as long as all desired species are in the neighborhood.

The opportunity for the Northeast and mid-Atlantic slam opportunity occurs from late summer through the end of the fall run. This happening most often takes place from the end of August right though mid-November, with heightened potential occurring in late September and October. The key to success is being able to target the migratory pelagic species that round out the slam. False albacore and Atlantic bonito will be the wildcards in this endeavor. While striped bass and bluefish frequent our waters for greater lengths of time, the window of opportunity for adding the bonito and false albacore to the slam is much smaller. Conditions must also be conducive for these seasonal visitors to make a prolonged stopover, thereby increasing the odds in your favor, and afforded a degree of predictability. In the Southeast, slam-eligible species tend to be available longer throughout the year. Obviously, the most important element in this equation is the presence of all four species at the same time and within reasonable proximity to one another.

Within the context of a typical Northeast season, Atlantic bonito will usually begin making an appearance during early August. The fish can show in great numbers or small schools. One of the keys for surf flyfishing success is the availability of silversides or spearing. While bonito will feed on various rainbait, anchovies, peanut bunker, and sand eels, I have found that the larger the spearing the better, and the longer the "bones" will hang around an area if they've zoned in on this bait source. Bonito are equipped with an impressive set of dentures so larger baits do not present a problem for them, and as a result they are quite willing to strike larger flies or other artificial baits.

False albacore usually greet Northeast inshore anglers sometime in late August, typically after the bonito have established themselves. Known also as fat alberts, albies, and hard tails, the false albacore especially prefer bay anchovies but are opportunistic feeders and will aggressively prey on peanut bunker and silversides as well. Finding the large masses of preferred bait in the surf zone is critical to finding concentrations of both albies and bones. With both species, the concentrations of preferred bait dictate where they will be and for how long. Bass and bluefish should be easiest of the four species to catch since, at this time of year, their feeding patterns have been established and their behaviors somewhat dependable. But bear in mind that easy in the context of fly fishing the surf is a relative term. Regardless of where you surf fish along the East Coast, and apart from the species sought, it is important to approach your day on the sand in search of the slam in a somewhat organized way.

The Strategy

No matter whether your hat trick or slam quest involves tarpon, bonefish, and permit, redfish, snook, and seatrout, or stripers, blues, and small tunas, it can be an exceptionally difficult thing to do from the beach. Anglers who enjoy consistent success at this game have acquired skills that only come with time on the water and constant learning. Most of my slam fishing has been in the Northeast, so I will use those experiences as the framework for a prototypical drill. Many of the elements of the strategy apply as well to mid-Atlantic and Southeast beaches. When pursing the Northeast slam, I make it a point to get out on the water early, usually before sunup. That way I can concentrate first on catching fish, usually bass, that are active during the morning hours in shallow water areas. I prefer to concentrate my efforts along sand and gravel beaches or in areas of mixed structure during the predawn and early morning hours. If you've patterned the bait and the bass and if luck is on your side, you could quickly eliminate that species from the list. One word of advice since I have been there: if you get into a good run of bass or any gamefish species for that matter, you will be tempted to hang around to keep catching. I know it is hard to leave fish to find other fish, but one of the tricks of successful slam fly anglers is to catch one species of fish and then quickly move on to the next. In my Northeast slam quest, I'd then target bluefish. Since they are quite prolific and very well entrenched in the area at this time of year, catching one should be a relatively easy thing to do— that is, if you don't encounter fish with selective lockjaw. Yes, even bluefish can on occasion get quite picky. But with a little persistence, the bluefish will get checked off the list in short order. Once again, if you do happen on some terrific blue fishing during this process, remember, catch one fish and get on to the next species!

Now comes the hard part. If you have been on the beach frequently enough, you just might be able to pattern the movements of the pelagics during various tide movements and times of the day. In areas that I fish I have seen the bonito get active soon after the sun rises. Therefore, I will target the bones for the triple, leaving the false albacore for the final leg of the slam. When present they will feed aggressively during the strongest portions of either tide. Often bonito and albacore will run together during the fall and if that occurs it makes the situation just a bit easier. But you know the old adage about "the best-laid plans of mice and men." Fish are the last thing on this earth to go with the day's plan, so my only other bit of advice is be adaptable and flexible and take what comes first. I've known some anglers who would even travel during the course of the day to reach beach areas where the particular species needed for the slam is most active, moving from spot to spot until they score. The small tunas are very fast swimming fish and can pop up one minute and be gone the next, traveling substantial distances as they feed. Some beach anglers have taken to chasing albies or bonito on foot as the fish bust bait on the surface and propel themselves in and out the water. It is inviting to take chase but my advice is that, unless you are training for a triathlon and need cardio conditioning, stay put. False albacore and bonito will often circle back to certain feeding stations that provide them with the best access to bait and to ambush points. This is when it pays to stop, look, and learn. Take a few moments to watch how the fish feed, move, and behave, and pick a spot where they seem to show most frequently. I once watched several large pods of albies feed well offshore of the beach. I watched them for well over an hour as they fed and moved in slow but steady direction toward the beach. After much observation I convinced myself that some of those fish would move well within casting range of the fly rod. I positioned myself along a sand bar that functioned to funnel baitfish to an irregular indentation along the shoreline. I waited and eventually the albies came; my patience rewarded with a hookup.

Similar beach strategies work well, regardless of where you fish slams, throughout the East Coast. Just take some time to plan your approach and the rewards can be yours.

Chapter Eleven

Destinations: An East Coast Surf-Fishing Journey

Our flyfishing tour of the East Coast begins in Maine and runs the course of the Atlantic seaboard, north to south, ending in Florida. Exceptional surf and wade fishing destinations are a hallmark of the East Coast of the United States. While there are many extraordinary locations where one can wet a fly line, our journey will encompass those places offering the best access and flyfishing opportunities.

So join me now as we travel from the Northeast regions of New England down to the southernmost tip of the United States.

Maine

The flyfishing journey begins along the rocky coastline of Maine that is a natural fish attractant. But it is the mid-coast and beach regions that draw the most interest among fly anglers. Maine's beaches cover approximately thirty miles of sand and surf that is suitable for wade and surf fly fishing. In addition to its beaches, Maine also offers wading opportunities throughout its harbors, bays and along portions of rivers where they join with the sea. Numerous tidal creeks and rivulets dot the landscape of the Maine coastline. Maine's primary coastline measures approximately 228 miles, but its entire tidal shoreline, which includes all nooks, crannies, fingers, points, etc. tallies almost 3,500 miles. While I have fly fished throughout Maine, it would take perhaps several lifetimes to cast a fly to all the potential fishy areas from Kittery to Eastport. To fully appreciate Maine's tidal-rich areas, take a look at a map and examine the geography that encompasses Freeport, Brunswick, Bath, Boothbay, and Bristol. That region of the state is filled with harbors, bays, coves, fingers of land, islands, points, and rivers. For the adventuresome fly angler these areas can offer countless wade fishing opportunities and a lifetime of exploration.

POINTS, CAPES, AND BEACHES

Kittery Point

Fort Foster Park at Kittery Point contains three small beaches. While the park's hours of operation may not coincide with the best fishing times, those beaches can be productive in the spring and fall months, and at dusk during the summer months. The Kittery region also includes shore flyfishing opportunities at Fort McClary, Fort Foster, and the popular Sea Point Beach.

Cape Neddick

This area is home to Cape Neddick Beach, also known as Passconaway Beach. The cape region hosts York Beach in Sohier Park and Long Sands Beach, situated halfway between York Harbor and York Beach. Long Sands contains about one and a half miles of ocean-facing beach.

York Harbor Beach

Also known as Mother's Beach, this stretch of sandy ocean front is situated along a rocky shoreline offering two forms of productive topography.

Cow Beach Point

The "point" is geologically a cape, and it is located in proximity to York Harbor. Like all land masses that jut into the ocean, this location has the potential to attract and hold bait and gamefish.

Short Sands Beach

This sandy beach is located in York Beach village and sits between rock cliffs. The beach is a small, quarter-of-a-mile stretch of sand that is in close proximity to the Nubble Light.

Ogunquit Beach

This is a peninsula sand beach that is one of Maine's most popular ocean-facing destinations. It is also a long beach that covers approximately three and a half miles of terrain for those anglers who like to wander off on their own.

Moody Beach

Located between Cape Neddick and Wells, this sandy beach is approximately a mile in length and extends from Moody Point to Ogunquit Beach. In addition to ocean fly fishing, the beach also offers access to back-area tidal marshes where kayak and wade opportunities are possible.

Wells Beach

Wells Beach provides some solid flyfishing opportunities for the wading angler and has a well-earned reputation for its good fishing. The area is a blend of sand beach and rocky shoreline, and the availability of jetty fishing is nearby at the mouth of the Webhannet River. Wells Beach has its own web cam and online weather station, so anglers interested in fishing this area can monitor beach conditions. Drakes Island Beach is also situated in the Wells area. It is a small sand beach and jetty configuration that sits between Wells and the Rachel Carson National Wildlife Refuge.

Crescent Beach

This beach is located approximately one half of a mile south of Wells Beach. Since it is one of the area's less-visited bathing beaches, it offers some degree of solitude for the fly angler.

Kennebunk Beach

Also known as Gooch's Beach, this is the longest section of the Kennebunk area beaches. Shore flyfishing opportunities abound along this portion of sand beach. Parsons Beach around the mouth of the Mousam River is an acknowledged honey hole for striped bass. The river banks around the Route 9 bridge also produce well, as do the jetties at the mouth of the Kennebunk River.

Colony Beach

This small stretch of sand beach is situated on Cape Arundel. While it may be small as far as beaches go, this location provides ease of access and a sense of seclusion. An adjacent jetty also offers flyfishing options.

Mother's Beach

This is yet another small, protected sand stretch that is part of the Kennebunk beaches. The beach is nestled in a sheltered cove that lies at the southern end of Kennebunk Beach.

Goose Rocks Beach

As you progress toward Kennebunkport you will encounter approximately three miles of sandy beach. The beach is somewhat protected from pounding waves by an offshore reef known as Goose Rocks. Barrier reefs of that nature are known to attract a wide assortment of gamefish that will find their way into the surf zone early, late in the day, and at night. Timber Island is located at the northern end of the beach.

Fortunes Rock Beach

Located in Biddeford, this ocean-facing sand beach extends for a length of about two miles from Biddeford Pool to Fortunes Rocks. The surf is relatively moderate and contains some good rips and rock zones that are ideal structure, especially for striped bass.

Biddeford Pool

This location is a large tidal pool of Saco Bay and south of the mouth of the Saco River. The rocky shoreline that rims the pool provides a number of flyfishing opportunities, as does the pool itself. When fishing from rocks it is always advisable to wear some form of traction cleats.

Hills Beach

This sand beach is located on the north side of Biddeford Pool and in proximity to the mouth of the Saco River. It runs for a length of about 500 yards and is surrounded by steep dunes. The area tends to hold a good diversity of forage with substantial numbers of sand eels. This is a good beach to fish very early or late in the day.

Camp Ellis

Camp Ellis Beach is situated at the mouth of the Saco River. Over time, the beach has been affected by the forces of nature resulting in significant erosion. As a result, the jetty and portions of the sea wall remain the only viable structure from which to fish.

Ferry Beach State Park

This diverse and natural parkland contains a classic ocean-facing sand beach that is ideal for surf fishing and in close proximity to the Saco River. There is a substantial amount of beach to explore and to cast flies from. This beach is one of the prettiest in the state and offers some great shoreline angling opportunities.

Bayview Beach

Bayview Beach is a small section of beach that is part of the larger expanse of contiguous beach and extends for almost seven miles around Saco Bay from Camp Ellis to Pine Point.

Old Orchard Beach

This is one of the oldest beaches in Maine and one of the most beautiful. Surf fishing is very actively pursued of the course of the beach's seven-mile expanse. The area offers shore fishing along three primary areas: Ocean Park; Surfside Beach; and the original Old Orchard Beach.

Pine Point Beach

Pine Point Beach is located in Scarborough and stretches four miles along a length of both Saco Bay and the Atlantic Ocean, and from the jetty at the mouth of the Scarborough River to Old Orchard Beach. The beach is also in close proximity to Maine's largest salt marsh.

Scarborough Beach State Park

Located in southern Maine, this is one of Maine's most popular beaches, since surrounding water maintains moderate temperatures throughout the summer and early fall. That condition is also conducive to holding bait and gamefish. The area is also known to have some formidable tidal rips. Scarborough Beach is also located close to the Scarborough River Jetty, known for its fine striped bass fishing.

Higgins Beach

This sand beach extends for more than one half of a mile, and is located near the mouth of the Spurwink River. This popular beach is a good bet for fly fishing for striped bass. Conditions, especially near the mouth of the river, will vary considerably depending on the river's water level and runoff from the watershed that results from higher than normal levels of rain.

Crescent Beach State Park

This ocean-facing sand beach is located in Cape Elizabeth and is recognized as an excellent surf-fishing location. The crescent-shaped beach stretches for about a mile and is considered by many to be representative of a typical and timeless saltwater ecosystem replete with sand dunes, beach grasses, and shore birds.

Two Lights State Park

This park is located in Cape Elizabeth. The location enjoys an excellent reputation for the quality of the surf fishing anglers can enjoy. The rocky shoreline and cliffs provide plenty of places for casting to the striped bass that frequent this area.

Popham Beach State Park

Popham Beach is one of Maine's best striped bass locations. The sand beach runs from the mouth of the Kennebec River, at Fort Popham, to the Morse River. While the strong surf makes this beach a difficult swimming beach, striped bass love to cruise areas where rips form in search of bait being swept by the currents. Exercise caution when wading. Fox Island is a good surf fishing spot at low tide, but anglers are warned to pay attention to the rising tides so as not to get marooned.

RIVERS AND BAYS

In addition to beach fishing, Maine is also home to many rivers, tidal creeks, and bays that offer the fly angler other excellent saltwater fishing opportunities. While that potential is vast, you can narrow down the possibilities with an Internet search or by a just grabbing a map and planning a flyfishing adventure. You just never know what gem of a spot you might find. Regardless of what that search may yield, there are a number of rivers and bays that are worth a stop on any angler's travels throughout the Pine Tree State.

Tidal sections: York River; Neddick River; Mousam River; Kennebunk River; Saco River; Fore River; Presumpscot River; Royal River; Harraseeket River; Androscoggin River; Kennebec River; Sheepscot River; Damariscotta River; Johns River; Casco Bay; Maquoit Bay; Middle Bay; Merrymeeting Bay.

New Hampshire

The surf-fishing opportunities within the state of New Hampshire are packed into a small length of real estate. The state contains approximately thirteen miles of ocean-facing coastline and about 131 miles of tidal shoreline. Several predominant beach areas and one large estuary comprise the mainstay shoreline flyfishing opportunities. The available sand beaches and rocky coastline provide for some excellent fishing for striped bass and bluefish.

Hampton Beach

This area is situated between Hampton and Seabrook. Hampton Beach State Park provides angling opportunities for bass and bluefish as does the area around the entrance to Harbor jetties. The inside reaches of the harbor are also good bets during the early part of the season.

Blackwater River

This tidal river is located in Seabrook and is a popular spot for striped bass fishing. As with most tidal rivers in the Northeast, the Blackwater is host to school-sized stripers. During the early season bass will be close to shore and dispersed within the marsh areas. As the river waters warm toward summer, bass will slide down toward the mouth of the river.

North Hampton State Beach

According to New Hampshire Fish and Game Department literature, this beach consistently produces some of the largest striped bass caught from shore each year in New Hampshire. As with other big bass locations, much of that harvest comes in the early morning or evening hours, two times that are ideal for the surf fly angler since that is a time when bass will venture close to shore and in range of a fly rod. Aside from the beach proper, areas of rocky shoreline, especially promontories, and rock outcropping can also be productive.

Rye Harbor State Park

This area is situated in Rye and lies between Jenness State Beach and Wallis Sands Beach. In addition to the sand beaches, the harbor jetties will offer the fly angler opportunities for striped bass. It is beneficial to use a high-density sink tip when fishing from this area since water currents moving in and out from the harbor can be significant and the sinking tip can help keep the fly near the bottom.

Great Island Common

This park is located in New Castle. Some of the area's most productive fishing occurs from the rocky shoreline or from the jetty. The area in and around the entrance to Portsmouth Harbor is a good location for striped bass.

Piscataqua River

This major river system flows to the Atlantic Ocean along with water from the Cocheco River, the Salmon Falls River, and the Little Bay. Anadromous fish species like shad and herring move into the river to spawn and striped bass follow them to feed. There are also a number of locations along the river that are worthy of the fly angler's time.

Goat Island Bridge

This bridge connects Great Island to Goat Island. The shoreline located on either side of the bridge can be productive for fly anglers during tidal movements at low light during the hours around dawn, dusk, and under the cover of darkness.

Bloody Point

The eddies and calm water of this section of river can be productive throughout the season and will hold bass during the summer. Fishing around rock structure adjacent to where those eddies form should also yield fish.

Hilton Park

This park is located at Dover Point and is adjacent to the General Sullivan Bridge. The park sits at the confluence of the Piscataqua River and Great Bay. Any location where two forms of water converge usually is a very productive fishing spot. First and foremost, baitfish will congregate in these areas and gamefish will follow.

Tossing flies from the rocks, along the bridge abutments, or around the pier can often bring results.

Great Bay

The Great Bay estuary encompasses a watershed of more than 6,000 acres and is the drainage basin for multiple area rivers: the Lamprey, Squamscott, Winnicut, Cocheco, Salmon Falls, and the Oyster rivers. This entire flow of water eventually feeds into the Piscataqua River. Great Bay is also a segment of the Gulf of Maine and is, therefore, part of a very rich ecosystem, one of the most fertile along the East Coast. Of interest to the fly angler are the miles of rocky shoreline, salt marshes, mud flats, tide waters, channels, and rivers that nurture baitfish and gamefish alike. Anadromous bait species like river herring move through this entire area to spawn and gamefish will be in hot pursuit. Some areas within this complex worthy of casting flies are: Scammell Bridge area between Dover and Durham. This is a good summer location that holds striped bass and some bluefish; Henry Law Park in Dover offers access to the Cocheco River that is host to substantial spawning runs of river herring throughout May and June; Newmarket Town Landing is known for harboring some large striped bass that venture to this area to feed on masses of river herring during spawning migrations.

Massachusetts

The Commonwealth of Massachusetts is geographically positioned to provide surf fly anglers with some of the best fishing opportunities the East Coast has to offer. From the waters that meet the coastal mainland to those that surround Cape Cod Bay, Buzzards Bay, Martha's Vineyard, and Nantucket, diversity of fishing opportunities are a hallmark of the Bay State. Massachusetts enjoys a coastline that is 192 miles long and a total tidal shoreline of about 3,500 miles. The Bay State is blessed with natural beaches. Cape Cod alone contains more than one hundred beaches, most of which are suitable for fly fishing. While there are literally too many fishable beaches and accessible tidal shorelines to list, the following will get you off to a good start.

State Marine Access Properties

In an effort to provide a continuing source of coast access opportunities for anglers, the state of Massachusetts has acquired a number of properties throughout the state that give anglers access to surf, pier, and jetty fishing. Current properties suitable for fly fishing are as follows: Craven's Landing at Scorton Creek, Sandwich; Popponesset Beach Shore Fishing Area, Mashpee; Leland Beach, Edgartown; Dogfish Bar, Aquinnah; Great Rock Bight Shore fishing area, Chilmark; Fore River Shore fishing area, Quincy.

CAPE COD

The Cape contains a wealth of beaches that are considered among the best surf-fishing beaches along the East Coast of the United States, in particular, those beaches that are a part of the Cape Cod National Seashore. The national seashore sits along the outer cape and embraces almost forty miles of ocean-facing sand beach. In aggregate tidal coastline, the CCNS encompasses almost 560 miles of well-preserved tidal shoreline. The National Seashore contains a blend of beaches, salt ponds, and tidal marshes, all suitable habitat to support a vibrant fishery.

The Cape is divided into four distinct segments: Outer Cape, Upper Cape, Mid-Cape, and Lower Cape. Within those segments are subsets of geography that includes: the Cape Cod National Seashore; the Bayside; Monomoy; the Southside; Buzzards Bay; and the Cape Cod Canal. Some of the more prominent angling locations on the Cape worthy of the angler's exploration are: Race Point off Provincetown; Pamet Beach near Truro; Wellfleet Harbor; Coast Guard Beach near Eastham; Nauset Beach; Stage Harbor near Chatham; West Dennis Beach; Craigville Beach; Dowses Beach; South Cape Beach; Woods Hole, Old Silver Beach and Wing Neck along Buzzards Bay; areas around the Bourne and Sagamore bridges; and on the Bay side—Scusset Beach, Sandy Neck, Barnstable Harbor; Chapin Beach; and Point of Rocks Beach. For more information about the Cape Cod beaches, visit www.capecodchamber.org/beaches.

Cape Cod Canal

The Cape Cod Canal deserves a special mention, since it is one of the most iconic and productive surf-fishing spots, not only in Massachusetts but along the entire East Coast. The canal divides the mainland from Cape Cod, and connects Buzzards Bay to the south with Cape Cod Bay to the north. The approximately seven miles of canal is affectionately known as The Big Ditch by those who regularly fish its shores for striped bass. Canal currents change directions every six hours and both cycles of water movement can be productive times to fish. Currents in the canal can be rather swift and can reach maximum speed of about five miles an hour. The canal is approximately 480 feet wide with a depth of between thirty and thirty-two feet. Most of the successful shore anglers fish the canal at night with conventional surf-fishing gear and large artificial plugs. One key to success when fly fishing the canal is to seek out currents lines, rips, eddies, holes, and troughs that occur close to shore and well within reach of a good cast.

Monomoy Island

Many surf fly anglers consider the eight miles of this island to offer some of the finest Northeast flats fishing for striped bass. Situated near Chatham, Massachusetts, the sand flats of Monomoy act as a magnet for cruising and feeding striped bass. Pristine sand beaches, wadable flats, and large striped bass make Monomoy a premier destination for fly anglers. One of the true gems of the Island is Monomoy National Wildlife Refuge, home to many species of marine life and wild life, including a plethora of baitfish, crustaceans, sea worms, mollusks, cephalopods, and juvenile fish species that gamefish prey upon. The sand flats north and south of Monomoy Island, Morris Island, and South Beach are areas that will provide plenty of fly angling opportunities. While fishing these flats, be mindful of channels, troughs, potholes, and deep water edges where bass will cruise or hold.

MARTHA'S VINEYARD

The Vineyard enjoys unique status as a true surf-fishing Mecca. For some anglers there is no finer fishing spot. Martha's Vineyard boasts about 125 miles of fishable shoreline that attracts striped bass, bluefish, Atlantic bonito, and little tunny. Strong currents in areas where the waters of the Atlantic Ocean and Nantucket collide are also favorite haunts for these gamefish. Some of the more prominent locations on the island are: Oak Bluffs; South Beach in Edgartown; Wasque Point; Cape Poge; Joseph Silva State Beach; Squibnocket Point; Chappaquiddick Beach; Gay Head; and Lobsterville Beach.

NANTUCKET

Given its name by native Americans, this "Far Away Land" attracts and holds legions of gamefish. The island is approximately thirty miles long and is located south of Cape Cod along with its sister islands, Tuckernuck and Muskeget. Striped bass, bluefish, Atlantic bonito, and false albacore make up the core of available fly-rod species. Sand beaches, backwaters, and flats offer a diversity of angling experiences. A few of the Island's angling hotspots are: the Bonito Bar near Tuckernuck; Brant Point; Eel Point; Great Point; Surfside Beach; and Smith Point.

BAYS AND HARBORS

The shorelines of bays and harbors can be productive places to fish and Massachusetts is blessed with a wealth of such fish-holding locations. I've enjoyed some of my finest fly fishing in the backs of harbors and wandering the shoreline of bays. Bays like Buzzards Bay and Cape Cod Bay are prime examples of locations that can deliver world-class fly angling results.

Boston Bay/Boston Harbor

The Boston Harbor Islands National Recreation Area is accessible via ferry, private boats, and kayaks. Once on the island, wade the shorelines. Islands that can be fly-fished are: Bumpkin, Gallops, Georges, Great Brewster, Grape, Lovells, and Peddocks. Other productive locations include the Winthrop shoreline, World's End Peninsula, and Castle Island. Although outside the boundaries of Boston Bay and Boston Harbor, both the North and South Shores of the Boston area also provide many angling opportunities. The North Shore contains the following: Marblehead, Devereaux Beach, Crane Beach, Plum Island, Joppa Flats, and Salisbury Beach State Reservation. Moving to the South Shore, some solid fly fishing can be found at: Scituate Harbor, Peggotty Beach, Humarock Beach, Rexhame Beach, Ocean Bluff, Duxbury Beach, Kingston Bay, Plymouth Harbor, and Plymouth Beach.

Gloucester

Although Gloucester is recognized as one of the most important ports and commercial maritime centers in the Unites States, its beaches can provide excellent opportunities for fly anglers. The following are some of the places to explore in the Gloucester area: Cressy's Beach at the end of Historic Stage Fort Park; Good Harbor Beach, a sand, ocean-facing beach; Half Moon Beach in Stage Fort Park; Niles Beach in East Gloucester and Pavilion Beach can produce results, but vehicle parking is limited; Plum Cove Beach, a small, intimate beach with limited parking; and Wingaersheek Beach, an ample stretch of beach close to the Annisquam River and Ipswich Bay. A long exposed sandbar is a good wading location, but be aware of the tides, especially high water.

Elizabeth Islands

I've caught some of my largest striped bass on the fly around these islands. Although the majority of the islands are privately owned, two allow public access: Cuttyhunk and Penikese. Naushon Island has several areas that have been set aside for public access.

RIVERS

Massachusetts rivers, especially tidal rivers that empty in bays with connectivity to the ocean, are wonderful locations to fly fish. The mouths of such rivers and the lower brackish sections are typically the best places to fish. Many of these rivers also seasonally host anadromous gamefish species such as striped bass and shad. The larger and more extensive river systems like the following often offer the best angling opportunities, but don't neglect some of Massachusetts' smaller rivers and tidal creeks: Connecticut River, Housatonic River, Merrimack River, Charles River, Deerfield River, Hoosic River, Quinnebaug River, Westfield River, Millers River, and the Blackstone River.

BEACHES

Many outstanding beaches mark the landscape of Massachusetts. The following are but a sampling of locations that can offer access to flyfishing opportunities. Typically the spring and fall months offer greater ease of fishing since summer beach crowds are not present at those times. That does not preclude some great summer fishing around early morning, dusk, and evening hours.

Cahoon Hollow Beach

The beach is approximately three miles from Wellfleet, Massachusetts and in proximity to Cahoon Hollow. The angler can expect to encounter striped bass, bluefish, summer flounder, and the occasional little tunny or false albacore.

Chapin Memorial Beach

This beach is located in Dennis, about two miles from Yarmouth. Fishing for striped bass can be done from the beach and from the adjacent flats that extend for more than a mile at low tide.

Cisco Beach

Cisco Beach is situated approximately four miles from Nantucket and is in proximity to both Hammond Pond and Clark Cove. This beach is well located for good surf fishing.

Coast Guard Beach

Located approximately two miles from Eastham. It is considered one of the area's nicest beaches and an excellent stretch of sand for fishing, especially for striped bass and bluefish.

Crane Beach

Located in Ipswich, this beach and adjoining sand flats can produce excellent fishing for striped bass. Fly fishing the flats, eddies, and current seams when bass are feeding on sand eels and bunker can be very productive. Other locations in the area worth prospecting are Hog Island, Fox Creek, and Coffin's Beach.

Devereaux Beach

Situated near Marblehead and Swampscott, Devereaux is considered a fine surf-fishing beach for striped bass. The area is known to attract prolific numbers of school-sized bass and larger specimens. As with many other similar beaches, anglers will find more solitude during the off season.

Duxbury Beach

This is a six-mile-long barrier beach situated along Marshfield to Gurnet Point, and to Saquish in the south. Nearby Duxbury Bay is a popular flats fishing area for shallow water striped bass and bluefish.

First Encounter Beach

Located approximately one and a half miles from Eastham, First Encounter Beach is another stretch of ocean-facing shoreline where the fly angler can catch striped bass and bluefish.

Humarock Beach

Situated on Cape Cod Bay in Scituate, the beach is located about three miles from Marshfield Hills. Striped bass and bluefish are the primary quarry with a seasonal abundance of midsized fish of both species. Wading access to the beach is via watercraft or the Marshfield town bridge.

Head of the Meadow Beach

This beach is located in North Truro and is one of the many beaches that are a part of the Cape Cod National Seashore. As with those other beaches, fishing at Head of the Meadow can be quite good for striped bass. Piping plovers also love the beach, so check any periodic closures during breeding season.

Horseneck Beach State Reservation

Located in Westport at the western end of Buzzards Bay, this two-mile-long barrier beach also contains a fertile salt marsh and encompasses approximately 600 acres. The combined habitats of sand beach, salt marsh, and estuary are ideal for attracting and holding both baitfish and gamefish.

Katama Beach

Katama Beach and Katama Bay on Martha's Vineyard are both great places to fish for striped bass and bluefish. While the beach is ocean-facing, the bay offers access to wadable flats where anglers can sight-cast to cruising bass.

Long Beach

Long Beach is one of Rockport's longer stretches of ocean-facing sand beaches good for surf fishing. A number of other smaller Rockport beaches are also in proximity to Long Beach and they too are worth exploring: Back Beach; Cape Hedge Beach; Front Beach; Old Garden Beach; and Pebble Beach.

Madaket Beach

This expansive beach is on Nantucket's west coast. Although it is a popular spot for beach goers, the extreme west end of the beach is accessible only with four-wheel-drive vehicles. Striped bass and bluefish will move along the nearshore areas during sunrise, morning, and sunset time frames.

Menemsha Beach

This delightful public beach is located next to Menemsha Harbor and is in proximity to Menemsha Pond and the Vineyard Sound. As with other area beaches, this is a good beach for striped bass and bluefish.

Nantasket Beach

Located in Hull, this sand beach is part of the Nantasket Beach Reservation, which encompasses almost twenty-six acres and 1.3 miles of ocean-facing shoreline. Numerous tidal pools also form at low tide.

Cisco Beach

The beach is located on Nantucket. It's an open beach with strong currents and rips, just the kind of conditions large striped bass gravitate toward.

Nauset Beach

Located in East Orleans, Nauset Beach offers access to numerous other beaches on the backside of the ocean. The northern section of beach to Nauset Inlet and Nauset Harbor is a favorite location for surf anglers chasing striped bass and bluefish.

Old Silver Beach

This Falmouth beach is easily accessible from Boston. The beach is a popular summer bathing spot, so some of the best angling solitude comes during the off season. A tidal creek divides the beach in two sections: one for residents and the other for visitors.

Race Point Beach

This beach is located in Provincetown at the tip of the Cape and is part of the National Seashore. The beach's topography and currents work to create excellent surf-fishing opportunities. Beach access via vehicle is allowed with the purchase of a seasonal permit.

Singing Beach

This beach is located in Manchester-by-the-Sea and is best known for its beauty and "singing" or squeaking sand. The beach is also known for the quality of its striped bass fishing, especially in the fall.

Rhode Island

Known as "The Ocean State," Rhode Island has a long and storied history as a premier surf-fishing destination. With forty miles of coastline and 384 miles of tidal shoreline, Rhode Island boasts some of the most iconic saltwater fishing locations along the East Coast. Relative to its geographic size, Rhode Island is blessed with an abundance of salty H_2O. Almost fifteen percent of its total physical area is comprised of numerous bays and inlets. In essence, Rhode Island is a small state with abundant surf-fishing opportunities along beaches, in parks, and in reserves, and through various small access points situated throughout the state. For a more detailed discussion of access points, please refer to the Rhode Island Surf Access Guide, a collaborative effort between Rhode Island Sea Grant, the Coastal Resources Center, and the University of Rhode Island. You can view the guide online at http://seagrant.gso.uri.edu/daytrip/pdfs/access_guide.pdf.

Block Island

Block Island is located about fourteen miles east of Montauk Point, New York and thirteen miles south of Rhode Island. That one-mile difference has given Rhode Island claim to this iconic fishing spot that has been hailed as one of The Last Great Places. That moniker is true in terms of history, physical beauty, and fishing that has been a part of the island's culture since the days of the Niantic and Narragansett Indians. Blessed with an abundance of flora and fauna, Block Island also contains many productive access points for exceptional surf fishing: Block Island National Wildlife Refuge, specifically Sandy Point and the shoreline in proximity to the North Lighthouse; Mansion Road Access; Mohegan Bluffs; Southwest Point; Charleston Beach; New Shoreham Coast Guard Station; Indian Head Neck Road; the area around the Ocean Avenue Bridge; Mosquito Beach; Andy's Way access; West Beach Road access to the Great Salt Pond; Southwest Light; Black Rock Point. The Great Salt Pond, an enclosed body of water, is located on Block Island. The pond is connected to Block Island Sound and divides the Island into north and south regions.

Westerly

The shorelines around Westerly are home to some of the most storied surf-fishing waters in Rhode Island. I've enjoyed some of my finest and most memorable striped bass fishing from the waters around the Watch Hill area. Bluefish are also plentiful in this region of the state as are seasonal pelagic visitors like Atlantic bonito and little tunny. At various times of the year prolific stocks of baitfish and gamefish will set up shop for an extended period. A few areas worthy of a fly rodder's cast are: the Pawcatuck River; Napatree Point; Watch Hill Light; Misquamicut State Beach; New Westerly Town Beach; Weekapaug Point; and Breachway.

Charlestown

Located in Washington County, Charlestown offers excellent access to a number of quality fishing spots for bass, bluefish, shad, weakfish, and small pelagic species. Some of the more accessible locations are: Quonochontaug Breachway; Blue Shutters Town Beach; East Beach; Charlestown Breachway; Charlestown Town Beach; Pen Creek Access; Ninegret Wildlife Refuge; Green Hill Beach; and Moonstone Beach.

South Kingston and Narragansett

Both South Kingston and Narragansett are located in Washington County. South Kingston incorporates a number of villages within its territory, while Narragansett runs along the eastern bank of the Pettaquamscutt River. This combined area embraces many fine areas to wet a fly line. Some of the high-profile areas include: South Kingston Town Beach; Deep Hole Fishing Area; Matunuck Management Area that includes the Ocean Avenue access and Matunuck State Beach; Fisherman's Memorial State Park; Galilee Bird Sanctuary; Bluff Hill Cove tidal flats; Salty Brine State Park; Roger Wheeler State Beach; Point Judith State Park and the Point Judith Light; Scarborough State Beach; Black Point; Bass Rock Road Access; Newton Ave. Access; Narragansett Town Beach; Narrow River Inlet; Old Sprague Bridge; the Pettaquamscutt Cove National Wildlife Refuge; and the South Ferry Road Access.

Jamestown/North Kingstown

These two towns are located respectively in Newport County and Washington County. Jamestown is a part of Conanicut Island, located in Narragansett Bay. The area contains some noteworthy surf-fishing locations: Seaside Beach; Petter Cove and Taylor Point; Sheffield Cove Marsh; Gilbert Stuart Road; Chafee Nature Preserve; Bissel Cove; North Kingstown Town Beach; and Compass Rose Beach.

Warwick

Warwick is the second largest city in Rhode Island and is located in Kent County. Its beaches are popular destinations for fly anglers. Some of the productive locations around Warwick include: Seaview Beach; Oakland Beach; Long Meadow Fishing Area; Conimicut Point Recreation Area; and the George Salter Grove.

Barrington

Barrington is often considered one of the best places to live in the United States. It is also one of the best places to fish in the state of Rhode Island and is located about nine miles southeast of Providence. The Warren River sits to the east of Barrington, and Narragansett Bay lies to the south and west. Given its geographic position all of Barrington sits no farther than about two miles from salt water. Some of those locations include: Haines Memorial Park; Nyatt/Dunis Access Road; Knockum Hill Reserve; and the Barrington Town Beach.

Warren

The town of Warren is located in Bristol County. Two of the more popular access points for surf fishing are the Warren Town Beach and the Barker Avenue access.

Bristol

Bristol is often referred to as the most patriotic town in the United States but it is also one of Rhode Island's most prominent maritime centers. Fine surf fishing can be found at a number of Bristol locations: East Bay Bicycle Path; Bristol Town Beach; Colt State Park; Mount Hope Fishing Access; Annawamscutt Drive Access; and the Narrows Fishing Area.

Portsmouth

Portsmouth is a part of Newport County and is a part of Aquidneck Island. The town covers a range of about sixty square miles, thirty-six miles of which are in the form of water. Portsmouth in total also includes Prudence Island, Patience Island Hope Island, and Hog island. Two of the more popular fishing areas are the Narragansett Bay National Estuarine Reserve and the McCorrie Lane Fishing Reserve.

Tiverton/Little Compton

The town of Tiverton is situated on the eastern shore of Narragansett Bay, near the Sakonnet River and Aquidneck Island. The adjacent town of Little Compton is located between the Sakonnet River and the Massachusetts state line. Some of the more accessible places to cast a fly are: the Sakonnet Bridge access; Grinnell's Beach; Seapowet Marsh; Fogland Beach; Sakonnet Harbor; South Shore Beach; Atlantic Beach; Sachuest Point National Wildlife Refuge.

Newport

Newport is known worldwide for its mansions but this resort town on Aquidneck is also a place a fly angler can pursue all suitable inshore gamefish. Places worth spending some time are: Goat Island Connection; Rose Island/Fort Hamilton; Brenton Point State Park; Kings Beach; Gooseberry Beach; and Easton's Beach.

Connecticut

The state of Connecticut is blessed with an abundance of wonderful inshore flyfishing possibilities. Predominant among those are the surf and wading opportunities along the beaches and backwaters of the Long Island Sound that extend from the town of Greenwich to Stonington. The amount of that tidal shoreline represents approximately 618 miles. Anglers fishing western Connecticut are also within striking distance of areas that border New York, for example Rye and Eastchester Bay. The freshwater rivers that flow into the Sound also offer excellent and consistent fishing throughout the season and nurture the anadromous species that spend time both in those rivers and in the open sound. Most of the premier inshore species of gamefish frequent this region. Striped bass and bluefish are abundant, summer flounder are very available, as are Atlantic bonito and little tunny in season. Fly anglers can also target shad and tempt some bottom-dwelling species like scup and tautog with flies. The Connecticut shoreline that runs along the length of the Long Island Sound is the primary area for fly anglers to wade as are the tidal stretches of the rivers that empty into the Sound. Most of these rivers will also host sizable numbers of small to school-sized striped bass throughout the year. These are resident bass that spend the colder months deep in to the rivers, and exit back into the Sound during the spring. The mouths of Connecticut rivers are also good locations to prospect for "sea run" trout that migrate from the rivers, into the Sound and then back upstream. The diversity of Connecticut's saltwater fishing will keep any fly angler busy with many opportunities.

CONNECTICUT STATE PARKS

Connecticut has a number of state parks that offer access to areas along the Long Island Sound. Many of these locations provide parking and other amenities and are great places to experience wade fly fishing. The following parks make available those opportunities: Bluff Point State Park, Groton; Fort Trumbull State Park, New London; Ferry Landing State Park, Old Lyme; Hammonasset Beach State Park, Madison; Harkness Memorial State Park, Waterford; Rocky Neck State Park, Niantic; Sherwood Island State Park, Westport; and Silver Sands State Park/Charles Island in Milford.

Town Access Locations

Many of the towns and villages that line the Long Island Sound shoreline offer access to beaches that can be fished. In each instance access regulations should be checked. Although the towns allow nonresident access, some beaches are for resident-use only.

- Branford: Town Beach; Branford Point; and Stony Creek Beach.
- Bridgeport: Saint Mary's By the Sea Beach; Seaside Park.
- Clinton: Clinton Landing.
- Darien: Pear Tree Point Beach; Weed Beach.
- East Haven: Farmington River State Park.
- East Lyme: Hole-in-the-Wall Beach; McCook Park; Railroad Beach; and Rocky Neck State Park.
- Essex: Bushnell Park; Essex Town Park; and Turtle Creek Wildlife Sanctuary.
- Fairfield: Jennings Beach; Penfield Beach; Penfield Reef; and Rickards Beach.
- Groton: Bluff Point State Park and Reserve; Eastern Point Beach; Guilford; East River Preserve; Great harbor Wildlife Management Area; and the Trolley Road Coastal Access.
- Lyme: Selden Neck State Park.
- Madison: East Wharf Beach; Hammonasset Beach State Park; and West Wharf Beach.
- Milford: Connecticut Audubon Coastal Center; Gulf Beach; Silver Sands State Park; Stewart B. McKinney National Wildlife Refuge; and Walnut Beach.
- New Haven: East Shore Park; and West River Memorial Park.
- Norwalk: Calf Pasture Beach; Shea/Ram Island; and The Plains Island.
- Norwich: Howard T. Brown Park.
- Old Lyme: Great Island Wildlife Management Area; Soundview Beach; Watch Rock Park.
- Preston: Poquentanuck Cove.
- Stamford: Cove Island Park; Cummings Park.
- Stonington: Barn Island Wildlife Management Area; Stonington Point.
- Stratford: Long Beach; Point-No-Point; Russian Beach; and Short Beach.
- Waterford: Jordan Cove; Baybrook Beach; Bradley Point; Dawson Ave. Beach; Morse Beach; Oak St. Beach; and Peck Beach.
- West Haven: Sandy Point and Sandy Point Bird Sanctuary; Seabluff Beach; and South St. Beach.
- Westport: Burying Hill Beach and Wetlands; Cockenoe Island; Compo Beach; Sherwood Island State Park; and Saugatuck River Access.

For further information please refer to the Connecticut Coastal Access Guide.

Long Island, New York

Long Island is considered one of the premier surf-fishing destinations in the entire United States. Fly anglers have been cashing in on excellent angling opportunities for quite some time. The Long Island coastline stretches for approximately 127 miles, with a total tidal shoreline of about 1,850 miles. This region's ocean-facing beaches are part of the Island's south shore, while the Long Island Sound provides an almost additional 120 miles of interior shoreline, with other tidal wade-fishing prospects present throughout harbor, bays, and creeks. The easternmost appendages of Long Island are referred to as the Forks. The terminal point of the north shore is Orient Point while the end of the south shore is Montauk Point, a recognized surf-fishing capital of the East Coast.

THE SOUTH SHORE

The South Shore of Long Island is positioned off the Atlantic Ocean and runs a course through Nassau County and Suffolk Counties and out to the fabled waters of Montauk. Most of the key locations along this entire length of shoreline are well known in the annals of Northeast sport fishing, and most of these same areas have steadily gained reputations as premier flyfishing destinations. A diversity of conditions on the South Shore offers the fly rodder a wealth of opportunities from ocean beach fishing to back bay, flat, inlet, and jetty angling. Many of the South Shore flats offer excellent sight fishing for striped bass.

Most of the areas listed here, while accessible to nonresidents, do have certain limitations and restrictions such as permit requirements, parking fees, and limited hours of operations. Before visiting an area, you should contact the particular venue for conditions of use.

Lido Beach

This small barrier island contains a fine stretch of beach that offers public access, except for a private stretch of beach known as the Dunes.

Jones Beach State Park

One of the first major fishing areas of Long Island's South Shore is Jones Beach State Park. The park consists of about 2,413 acres and is positioned with access to almost six and a half miles of beach. The relatively undeveloped west-end portion of the park offers some excellent surf fishing, but the entire beach can deliver outstanding fly fishing throughout the season. The area is also the beneficiary of significant numbers of migratory fish during the fall run, most prevalent being striped bass, bluefish, and false albacore. The adjacent and contiguous areas of Tobay Beach, Gilgo Beach, Gilgo State Park, and Oak Beach offer fine fly rodding as well. Areas on the backside of Jones Beach, such as Zach's Bay and all of the islets of South Oyster Bay, provide a wealth of angling exploration opportunities.

Fire Island National Seashore

This expansive natural resource is owned and managed by the National Park Service and embraces almost twenty-six miles of ocean-facing beach, most of which can be quite productive fly water in season. Fire Island is bracketed by Democrat Point on the west and Moriches on the east. The western boundary begins with Robert Moses State Park. This park has approximately five miles of ocean-facing beach from which surf-fishing fly anglers can wade and cast. The eastern fringe of the park is contiguous with the Fire Island National Seashore.

The Island is a barrier situated between the Great South Bay and the Atlantic Ocean. The area offers some of the best and most diverse flyfishing opportunities you will find anywhere on Long Island. The beaches around Fire Island Inlet attract and hold striped bass, bluefish, and weakfish for most of the season. It is a consistent location from the spring months right through the fall run. The Sore Thumb is one of the most recognized and productive fishing spots in the area around the Inlet, especially for striped bass. Fire Island Inlet has very turbulent and fast moving currents and all caution should be exercised when fishing from a boat or wading.

Many of the backwater islands, cuts, channels, flats, salt marshes, and coves are very much worth the time to explore them. The beaches within the vast expanse of this national seashore area can produce results throughout the entire course of its range. Smith Point County Park at the eastern tip of the seashore is a very popular place to surf fish. The park allows four-wheel driving on the outer beach with the appropriate permit and equipment. Smith Point Beach is a quite productive location during the fall migration.

Great South Bay

The Great South Bay is the largest shallow bay of its kind in the State of New York. It encompasses approximately 64,000 acres with a total area of 150,000 square miles and is positioned between Moriches Bay to the east and South Oyster Bay to the west. The area contains an ecosystem of islands, salt marshes, tidal flats, eelgrass beds, rivers, creeks, channel cuts, and dredges and still-undeveloped real estate. The waters technically create a massive back-barrier lagoon that is home to a wide diversity of gamefish. The shallow water nature of the bay is ideally suited to the fly angler. Six significant bodies of flowing water are part of the Bay's watershed: Beaverdam Creek, Carmans River, Connetquot River, Champlin Creek, Orowoc Creek, and the Swan River. Fly fishing the flats of this area is a relatively new phenomenon but the opportunity is open-ended. This is truly one of the great bays of the Northeast.

Moriches Bay

The Moriches Bay ecosystem consists of a segment of barrier beach and a backwater bay and lagoon network. Moriches Bay is situated east of Great South Bay and west of Shinnecock Bay and encompasses the waters of Moneybogue Bay and Quantuck Bay. The varied habitat includes open water, salt marshes, islands, and flats. The watershed embraces almost fifteen square miles and is comprised of tidal creeks, marshes, and shoals. Moriches Bay is a very shallow body of water; much of its depth is six feet or less. The bay supports a vibrant fishery for striped bass, bluefish, shad, fluke, weakfish, and seasonally visiting pelagic species. The areas around Moriches Inlet are especially productive for large bass and false albacore.

Cupsogue Beach County Park

This beach lies just to the west of Moriches Inlet. This is a Suffolk County facility and embraces a 296-acre barrier beach park that offers ocean beach flyfishing opportunities. Striped bass and bluefish are the primary species encountered and the fishing during seasonal peaks can be excellent.

The Canals

Three canals on the South Shore of Long Island are worthy of the fly fisher's attention: the Quogue, Quantuck, and Shinnecock Canals. The first two link Moriches Bay with Shinnecock Bay, while the third is a conduit between the Shinnecock and Peconic Bays. Long Island canals are typically very productive fishing locations, especially during the early parts of the season. These three locations are known for their spring populations of flounder, bluefish, and striped bass.

Shinnecock Bay/Jetty/Inlet

The area around and including Shinnecock Bay is yet another quality flyfishing location. The almost twenty-four square-mile bay contains very diverse habitats: sand flats, tidal creeks, salt marshes, mud flats, sandy shoals, eel grass, and mussel beds. The shallow water areas of the bay are ideal areas for the fly rodder, especially the salt marshes and mudflats that border the barrier island, as are the locations around the tidal creek outlets. As an estuary, the entire bay is a fertile nursery to many species of fish. Shinnecock Inlet leads directly from the bay to the Atlantic Ocean; as a result the bay continually benefits from the ebb and flow of the tides.

Montauk

Montauk Point is the easternmost extremity of New York and fondly referred to as "The End." At the height of the fall run, the fishing has to be seen to be believed; at its best it is phenomenal. As with fishing anywhere, there are sometimes those days when wind and weather seem to conspire against the fly angler, but even then the persevering fisherman can still mount an acceptable outing and a memorable catch.

As prolific as the fishing is at Montauk, so too are the places one can fish. Montauk affords the fly angler options to fish sand beaches, rocky shorelines, and even back bay waters. Basically the area is divided into three sections—the North Side, the South Side, and The Point. Some of the more legendary locations are Ditch Plains, Gurney's, Hither Hills, Gin Beach, Culloden, Shagwon, Stepping Stones, North Bar, False Bar, The Bluffs, Turtle Cove, Dead Man's Cove, and of course The Point itself. A number of area parks provide access to excellent surf fishing. Those parks are: Camp Hero State Park, Hither Hills State Park, Montauk Point State Park, and Theodore Roosevelt County Park.

BETWEEN THE FORKS

Great Peconic Bay

Peconic Bay is positioned between the North and South Forks of Long Island. The western fringe, close to the Riverhead fork, includes Flanders Bay, Reeves Bay, and to the east the Little Peconic Bay, which sits somewhat between Southold and Sag Harbor. Robbins Island sits in the middle of this ecosystem and has been a prolific area for weakfish. This entire system is rich in tidal creeks and tidal ponds that empty into the network of bays and carry baitfish along with that flow. Moving further east and contiguous to Little Peconic Bay are Hog Neck Bay and Nassau Point.

Shelter Island and Vicinity

This 8,000-acre island sits sheltered between Gardiners Bay, Little Peconic Bay, Noyack Bay, Southold Bay, and Shelter Island Sound. Areas of fishing prominence are West Neck, Mashomac Point, Ram Island, Coecles Harbor, Hay Beach Point, and Jennings Point. Two tidal flows—Gardiners Creek and Chase Creek—are also noteworthy locations.

Gardiners Bay and Gardiners Island

Gardiners Bay is a small appendage of the Atlantic Ocean. It is approximately ten miles long and eight miles wide. The bay sits between the two easternmost ends of both the North and South Forks of Long Island—ideally situated for maximum fish traffic. The bay further lies in close proximity to Block Island and Shelter Island and connects to the Great Peconic Bay. The waters around Gardiners Island offer some of the finest sight fishing for striped bass that you will find anywhere on the

East Coast. The waters surrounding Gardiners Island are an ideal venue for sight casting the flats for striped bass.

The North Shore and North Fork

LONG ISLAND SOUND

The Long Island Sound is a large estuary situated between the north shore of Long Island, a portion of the Queens County shoreline, and the Connecticut coastline. For purposes of this book, the central zone of the Long Island Sound begins at about Eaton's Neck and the Nissequogue River and extends a little past Shoreham and Wading River. Points east of those locations are referred to as the North Fork with the terminal point being Orient Point. All the areas profiled are fundamentally affected by the same movements of baits and generally attract the same species of gamefish. Some areas of the Sound have greater proclivity toward attracting and holding bigger bass throughout the season, while other areas tend to appeal to school bass populations. For the most part, though, each area sees peak times when big fish move through. That is true for bass, bluefish, and to a lesser extent weakfish. Also, the pelagic species—bonito, false albacore, and Spanish mackerel—tend to make greater appearances in the central to eastern Sound areas. But fish are not always predictable and their patterns of travel often change from one year to the next.

WESTERN LONG ISLAND SOUND

Throgs Neck Bridge Area

The areas around the Throgs Neck Bridge represent the beginning of the western boundary of the Long Island Sound. These waters offer excellent early season opportunities for striped bass as the fish migrate out of the Hudson and East Rivers and into the Sound. The peninsula of Throgs Neck itself offers some fine angling, as do surrounding areas of the East River, Little Bay, Stepping Stones, and portions of Eastchester Bay.

Execution Light

While its name may have ominous and foreboding connotations, the fishing is far from that. When the resurgence in stripers began in the early 1990s, this was one of the first places that I remember cashing in on the revived bounty of bass. Since then it has only gotten better. The structure around the light is an ideal habitat for stripers. Its currents and depth changes can be quite conducive to fly fishing. This very rocky area is fishable from a boat.

City Island

I caught my first keeper striped bass in the waters of City Island many moons ago when the legal limit was a mere sixteen inches. I have not been back there in decades, but many of the same locations that I fished have been the beneficiary of the revival of Northeastern gamefish, principally the striped bass. For the fly angler, two of the best early season locations in the area are Turtle Cove and the waters around Hart Island.

Little Neck Bay

This is the perennial early season hot spot of the western Sound. The back portions of the bay consistently turn on with school stripers during mid to late April. The timing of this activity varies depending on the mildness or severity of the winter. The bay has an average depth of about six to eight feet and substantial tide movement of between seven to nine feet.

WESTERN NORTH SHORE HARBORS AND BAYS

The North Shore of Long Island is blessed with many harbors and bays, the product of a terminal moraine glacier that put on the brakes thousands of years ago. Most of these harbors exhibit similar attributes and traits that attract and hold fish. The harbors are very active in the early part of the season, April, May, and June, and then again in the fall months when the migration gets up a head of steam. Once the waters warm and the bait moves outside into the Sound, the fishing inside slows down, with the exception of early morning, evening, and nighttime fishing.

Manhasset Bay

Manhasset Bay is another productive early season location for stripers. Bluefish maintain a presence in the area throughout most of the summer. The bay gets active again with bass in the fall months. Some areas worth exploring are Plum Point, Toms Point, the entrance to Port Washington, Sands Point, Barker Point, and Half Moon Beach.

Hempstead Harbor

A number of coves and points highlight the flyfishing opportunities of Hempstead Harbor. This harbor is a good place to work off the effects of cabin fever, since it attracts not only large numbers of school-sized bass but its fair share of large bass as well. Each season some very big stripers are taken from this area. Some of the more popular areas inside the harbor are Bar Beach, Mott Point and Mott Cove, Crescent Beach, and Dosoris Creek.

Matinecock Point

While this point attracts stripers and bluefish, it is best known as a weakfish spot. With the rebounding of weakfish stocks, this area of late has seen more and more fly-rod catches of weakfish. While most are small, the area holds larger fish as well—some upwards of ten to twelve pounds.

Oyster Bay

This well-protected bay has some excellent fishing structure in the form of sunken barges and deepwater areas surrounded by shallow expanses. Oyster Bay Harbor, as well as West Harbor, offers the boating angler a number of flyfishing opportunities. The areas around Center Island, Cove Neck, Rocky Point, and Center Island Reef can produce fish in season as well. This region is especially productive in the spring. The shallowest parts of the harbors are very well suited to kayak fishing.

Cold Spring Harbor

The early season in this harbor finds a wealth of bait and striped bass spread throughout the entire area. The shallower lower portions of the lower bay heat up first in the spring and can make for some enjoyable fly fishing for school stripers. Later on in the season, bluefish dominate the fishing scene, and the lucky fly angler just might tempt a large tiderunner weakfish from these waters. As with other North Shore locations, rocks and boulders are a part of the land and waterscape.

Cold Spring Beach, Floyd Beach, Lloyd Point, and areas around the Sand Hole are favorite locations. Lloyd Neck is also home to Caumsett State Park, which is a favorite destination for local fly anglers. Another area worthy of exploration is Lloyd Harbor, tucked in between Cold Spring Harbor, Lloyd Neck, and West Neck. This entire area can be very productive.

Huntington and Northport Bays

The waters in and around both bays are excellent for the boating and wading fly angler. Two peninsula beaches—East Beach and West Beach—frame the opening to Huntington Bay and are ideally situated to attract all species of gamefish. Adjacent to West Beach and forming somewhat of a fork is Sand City, a very popular fishing hole. At the northern reaches of East Beach is Target Rock. The waters around this location are excellent as well. Located toward the back of Northport Harbor are Centerport Beach, Centerport Harbor, and Little Neck Point, all worthwhile fishing spots.

Eatons Neck

The Neck is the westernmost border of Smithtown Bay. This is an area that historically produces quite a number of large bass and bluefish. Bonito and false albacore also seasonally visit the area. While bait fishermen tend to have the most consistent success in this area, fly fishermen do quite well throughout the season. Two important sound-facing beaches in the area are Asharoken Beach and Crab Meadow Beach.

CENTRAL LONG ISLAND SOUND

Sunken Meadow State Park

Moving into the Town of Smithtown, the first major location of interest to the fly angler is the almost three-mile-long stretch of beach contained within Sunken Meadow State Park. The spring and fall months are prime periods to fish this beach, but excellent fishing reports emanate from this area throughout the entire season. The expanse of beach provides an opportunity to wander away from the crowds and to stake out a bit of one's own flyfishing solitude.

Smithtown Bay

Smithtown Bay is situated between the two prolific locations: Eatons Neck to the west and Crane Neck to the east. The Nissequogue River empties into the western end of the bay. The bay stretches for a length of approximately ten and a half nautical miles and attracts striped bass, bluefish, and false albacore. It is also an excellent area for fluke. Smithtown Bay contains varied fish holding structures and habitat, from sand beaches and rocky shoreline to deeper offshore humps and even an artificial reef. The bay also has a relatively extensive set of flats that offer sight-fishing opportunities for bass.

Nissequogue River

The Nissequogue has enjoyed a longstanding reputation for fine trout fishing. This portion of the river, which empties into the Long Island Sound, can be especially productive during the dropping tide. The outflow of water brings with it baitfish to the waiting predators stationed at the mouth of the river. The tidal section of the Nissequogue was one of the first areas on Long Island where striped bass were taken on the fly, by anglers fishing for sea run brown trout. Access to this area can be obtained through the Nissequogue River State Park.

Stony Brook Harbor and Porpoise Channel

These are both excellent flyfishing locations. Long Beach is a productive stretch as well—especially the section immediately adjacent to the harbor entrance. The backwaters of the harbor are a terrific spring location for striped bass and the myriad of backwater sloughs, drains, and grassy banks make for ideal fly fishing. Walking north and east toward Crane Neck will reveal a number of excellent areas that attract bass, bluefish, and false albacore. One very popular fly-rodding spot is West Meadow Beach. An extended sand bar runs adjacent to deeper water. Wading fly fishermen need pay particular attention to the rising tide before fishing this bar. You do not want to be stranded there at high tide.

Crane Neck

Crane Neck is located at the eastern end of Smithtown Bay. This boulder-strewn location is a magnet for striped bass. The gravel and sand beaches surrounding the Neck are also highly productive. Large bass and bluefish are consistently caught in this area, as are false albacore in the later summer months and during the fall run. Since most of the areas around the Neck are private property, the most viable fishing opportunities are by boat, but for those who gain access, the beach walk from Crane Neck to the western side of Flax Pond should yield fish.

Flax Pond

This tidal pond is located between Crane Neck and Old Field Point. While the pond itself is quite a productive place to fish, the areas where the pond drains into the Sound are where most of the action takes place. The rock structure around the mouth as well as the adjacent beaches to the east and west produce fish throughout the entire season. As the pond drains during the outgoing tide, a significant rip current develops that should be fished with caution.

Old Field Point

A lighthouse sits atop Old Field Point, with rock outcroppings and a boulder-strewn beach lying below. All of this acts as a magnet for striped bass and other gamefish. The area is replete with large boulders and rocks, remnants of the last glacial movements. Tidal and other current flows are affected by the large underwater boulders and rocks and, as such, tend to create productive rips and eddies. Most of the surrounding Old Field Beach areas rest on private property and wading access is limited.

Port Jefferson Harbor

"Port Jeff" is one of the most active harbors on Long Island. The surrounding areas of Port Jefferson get seasonal runs of various gamefish. The harbor itself, like so many other protected bays and backwaters, can be productive in the spring for striped bass. The area is best known for its phenomenal run of fluke, also known as summer flounder. During peak years, it is amazing how many of these flatfish are caught. They are a great fish to target with the fly rod, especially when in their shallow-water holding locations. Bluefish also consistently invade this area and range in size from small snappers to massive fish of over twenty pounds. During the very late summer and early fall, the fly angler might be treated to a run of false albacore as well, as they bulk up for their annual migration. Within the boundaries of the harbor are other areas worth exploring: Conscience Bay, Setauket Harbor, and Strongs Neck.

Mount Sinai Harbor

This is one of the most popular early season locations for striped bass. The harbor is a fertile and prolific fishery and acts as a nursery for many species of fish. In season, striped bass, bluefish, bonito, and false albacore frequent the harbor and its adjacent beaches. The inside of the harbor and its backwaters and salt marshes are productive early in the season and for as long as bait remains abundant. Mount Sinai Harbor is one of the first in the central Sound area to heat up in the spring, regarding both water temperature and fish activity. It is one of the most popular areas of the central North Shore, since it offers back bay, pier, and beach fishing opportunities.

Cedar Beach runs east from the east entrance of Mount Sinai Harbor. It is a very popular surf-fishing spot and is very fly fishing friendly. The harbor and beach consistently attract runs of false albacore.

MILLER PLACE/ROCKY POINT/SHOREHAM

Traveling east from Cedar Beach, you will come upon a number of excellent fishing locations. The entire continuum of beaches from Cedar Beach out to Shoreham has excellent flyfishing potential. Locations of particular interest to the fly angler are the beach off Miller Place, Woodhull Landing, Sound Beach, Rocky Point Landing, the beach off Rocky Point, Hallock Landing, and Shoreham Village beaches. These locations are also quite productive for striped bass during the night tides, hold bluefish throughout the entire season, and are visited seasonally by bonito and false albacore.

North Fork and East End

If you are an exploring type, this is a great area to scout either from the surf. Many of the same terrain and shoreline characteristics exist throughout the entire range of the area, and gamefish visit most of these locations at some time during the season.

MATTITUCK AND POINTS EAST

Moving north and east from the defined "fork" of Long Island at Riverhead is the first important North Fork location: Mattituck Inlet. The entrance to the inlet is located at James Creek. The areas around the inlet, including Cutchogue Harbor, offer fine angling. The small tidal backwater creeks of the harbor can be explored with flats style boats or kayaks. There are also numerous small inlets off the main channel leading from the inlet to the marina that also hold fish. This inlet gives the boating angler access to good fishing locations both to the east and west. The current flow at the inlet and in the channel can be quite strong, so small craft should be operated with caution.

Proceeding eastward, there are a number of locations that the fly fisherman should pay particular attention to. The first is Duck Pond Point, a promontory situated between rocky beaches to the west and east. This location can be good for striped bass during the early season and again in the fall. The entire stretch of rocky beach from Duck Pond Point out to Horton Point contains excellent striped bass water. When bluefish are present, they run the beaches most often during the early morning hours and again at dusk. Most of the beach access is through private or town property.

Continuing east, the next noteworthy spot to explore is Goldsmith Inlet. This outflow can produce excellent results with bass and late season false albacore and is best fished on the outgoing tide. The current movement out from the tidal pond brings with it bait and a water flow much like that of a small creek or river. In situations like this, I prefer to use an intermediate or high-density sink tip, especially if there are no visible signs of surface feeding activity.

Just east of Goldsmith and before Horton Point is Horton Lane Beach. This beach and Hashamomuck Beach, which is located between Horton Point and the town of Greenport, are two rocky beach expanses that attract a lot of gamefish. Striped bass, bluefish, and false albacore are frequent seasonal visitors. During some seasons the area also attracts migratory Spanish mackerel.

Greenport is one of the most interesting towns on the North Fork. It is also a great location from which to springboard either west or east for some outstanding fly fishing. Some great fishing can be had in the waters right off the town itself. From Greenport you are within striking distance of Orient Point and that magnificent fishery. The region from Greenport east is a striped bass haven, known for its large bass and bluefish. False albacore, bonito, and Spanish mackerel often migrate through this stretch of water in large numbers. The area also hosts large fluke and blackfish. Popular flyfishing locations in this area include Rocky Point, Truman Beach, Mulford Point, and Pettys Bight.

East End of North Fork

Orient Point is the easternmost tip of the North Fork. Like its counterpart on the South Fork, Montauk, it too is a fish attractor and offers fine angling throughout the entire course of the season, especially for striped bass and bluefish. It is a particularly astounding flyfishing location in the fall when bait and gamefish amass in the region during their migration south. Bonito, false albacore, Spanish mackerel, and small bluefin tuna all come within range of this North Fork "point." Surf fishing can be excellent. While this area produces some of the best angling results on Long Island, it also contains some of the most tumultuous and treacherous water to be found in the Northeast. This is especially true with the waters around The Race, Great and Little Gull Islands, and Plum Island. The turbulent conditions attract huge striped bass, but only experienced boating anglers should attempt to fish these waters. If you are new to the area, a number of excellent captains who cater to fly fishermen can put you in the red zone.

Orient Point State Park is a "fly-friendly" area from which one can beach fish, while the surrounding waters of Hallock Bay offer some scenic and quality fly fishing for the kayak angler. Long Beach, Orient Beach, and Orient Harbor are worth exploring as well.

NEW YORK CITY

It may come as a surprise to many, but the Big Apple and its boroughs have become synonymous with hot fly fishing. As local waters around the major metropolis have been given a chance to cleanse from many years of pollution and abuse, and with the resurgence of a variety of gamefish, New York City now provides many saltwater angling opportunities. While some of the best fishing is reached via boat, there is enough quality surf and wade fishing to satisfy the appetites of resident or visiting anglers.

STATEN ISLAND, BROOKLYN, AND QUEENS

The New York City boroughs of Staten Island, Brooklyn, and Queens are aquatically connected in many respects to the waters of Long Island. Most of the gamefish that move to more easterly regions of Long Island begin their early season activity in these westerly zones. Staten Island has come into its own as a wade fishing destination. Of particular interest to shore bound fly anglers are the beaches of Great Kills and the Gateway National Recreational Area. Another popular area is South Beach, not to be confused with the beach of a similar name famous for its diet. This South Beach has a two and a half-mile boardwalk that runs parallel to its length. While the beach area can get quite crowded during the height of the summer, it is a good early and late season destination for the fly rodder.

Staten Island

Conference House Park

As a New York City-owned facility, this location offers opportunities for beach fishing and allows for the use of hand-launched boats. Located at the west end of Hylan Boulevard, the Park is at the southerly end of Staten Island and adjacent to the waters of Raritan Bay.

Mount Loretto

The state of New York provides access to this location. It offers surf fishing from sandy and rocky beaches situated off the waters of Raritan Bay.

Dorothy Fitzpatrick Fishing Pier

While primarily for pier fishing, this location offers access to beach fishing as well. It is located in the region of Prince's Bay. Hand-launched boats are permitted. Access is provided by the City of New York.

Lemon Creek Park

Located in the upper portion of Prince's Bay, this city park offers the fly angler access to rocky beach surf angling.

Wolfe's Pond Park

A fishable sandy beach is the primary attraction for fly anglers in this city park. It is well positioned to fish the seasonally productive waters of the Raritan Bay. The small freshwater pond is popular for largemouth bass fishing.

Crescent Beach Park

This access area is owned by New York City and offers sandy and rocky beach fishing opportunities. Hand-launched boats are permitted.

Crooke's Point

This area is located in Great Kills; access is provided through the National Park Service. The primary fishing environment is that of sandy beach. There is also a stretch of open beach located between Crooke's Point and the beginning of the Gateway National Recreational Area that offers surf opportunities for the fly rodder.

FDR Boardwalk

Situated from Miller Field to Fort Wadsworth, the boardwalk offers access to both sandy and rocky beach surf fishing, and jetty fishing. This facility is operated by New York City.

Snug Harbor

City access to rocky beach and steep shoreline fishing. This area is also in the general location of the Kill Van Kull and close to the Staten Island Botanical Gardens.

West End of Victory Boulevard

With New York City access and marshy shoreline, this can be an interesting place to prospect in the early part of the season, when grass shrimp and other crustaceans attract early season stripers and weakfish. Hand-launched boats are permitted.

Brooklyn

There was a time in the history of New York City when the maritime areas around Brooklyn hosted an exceptionally productive fishery, especially for striped bass. As a matter of angling record, Brooklyn contained some of the then best "go-to" locations for trophy bass to be found anywhere in the Northeast. To the enjoyment of most fishermen who frequent these locations, and in particular the many fly anglers, there has been a revival of those heyday runs. Anglers fishing out of Brooklyn today have relatively easy access to the 9,155-acre Jamaica Bay Wildlife Refuge, which is part of the even larger 26,000-acre Gateway National Recreational Area. This massive park contains some of the more notable areas that now attract the interest of local and visiting fly fishermen are: Rockaway Inlet, Sheepshead Bay, Manhattan Beach, locations around the Marine Parkway Bridge, Upper and Lower New York Bays, and Coney Island Beach. The area boasts a considerable stretch of productive beach that can be explored and prospected by the more adventurous surf and boat anglers.

Jamaica Bay

The Jamaica Bay Wildlife Refuge is part of the Gateway National Recreational Area. It is one of the most significant such urban refuges in the country. Each of three New York City boroughs lay claim to portions of the Bay. As such an important fishery, it has been included in each discussion of urban flyfishing potential. This perennial early and late season hotspot can remain active throughout the entire season for the complete range of local, migratory, and pelagic species, and can be especially productive for large striped bass on bunker flies when menhaden are available. If conditions remain conducive, bunker can reside in the bay and surrounding areas for most of the season. But the big bass and weakfish move on once the water temperatures rise outside their preferred temperature zone. Then the blitzing bluefish become the mainstay species. The area is also a popular destination for the highly coveted little tunny.

Within Jamaica Bay and within reach of boating fly anglers are areas such as North Channel, Grassy Bay, Pumpkin Patch Channel, Runaway Channel, and Beach Channel. The area has also become a favorite location for kayak fly anglers due to the smaller creeks, bays, and backwaters contained within the boundaries of the larger area. Shore-bound anglers also have number of options available to them as well.

Canarsie Park

Managed by the National Park Service, this park offers the opportunity for beach and pier angling. For the fly angler, the sand beach area is of primary importance. It is situated in the more southerly portion of Jamaica Bay.

Floyd Bennett Field

This is another National Park Service facility with access in proximity to the Marine Parkway Bridge. Primarily an area of rocky and sandy beach. Access to this area is offered on a twenty-four hour basis with a permit.

Plum Beach

This is an ideally situated beach for fly anglers. It runs along a promontory that juts into the Rockaway Inlet and is bordered by Marine Parkway Bridge, Sheepshead Bay, and Manhattan Beach. This is a relatively large beach area and the newcomer might benefit from the services of a local guide.

Sheepshead Bay

Within this bay are a number of city-owned facilities. While not ideally suited for fly fishing, they offer some angling opportunities if you happen to be in the neighborhood. Those locations are: Brigham Street Bulkhead, Sheepshead Piers, the Foot Bridge, and Shore Boulevard. The fishing here ranges from pier and bulkhead fishing to limited beach fishing.

Brooklyn West

The waters of the Upper and Lower New York Bays dominate the western sections of Brooklyn. There are quite a few access points here that afford contact with the waters of both bays: Coney Island Beach and Creek Park, primarily sandy beach fishing; Kaiser Park, beach and pier fishing; Dreier-Offerman Park, beach fishing; Lois Valentino Park, shoreline fishing; and the Empire–Fulton Ferry State Park, rock beach and bulkhead fishing.

Queens

The borough of Queens offers some varied fishing opportunities. The Rockaways portion of this area is well positioned to take full advantage of the waters of Jamaica Bay and the Gateway National Recreational Area. A significant portion of the park is located in Queens, and the more northerly reaches of the borough offer access for the Long Island Sound, Flushing Bay, Little Neck Bay, and the upper portion of the East River. Collectively, these waters offer quite diverse flyfishing opportunities and tend to get active early in the season and hold fish throughout the year, once again reaching a second peak in the fall months.

Beginning with the waters of Jamaica Bay and the Gateway National Recreational Area, there are numbers of beach, bay, and marsh areas to explore either via wading, boat, or kayak. Some of the more noteworthy areas within the Bay are Pumpkin Patch Channel, Black Wall Channel, Grassy Hassock Channel, Broad Channel, Horse Channel, and Head of Bay. There are also a plethora of nooks and crannies, basins, tidal ponds, and creeks in this area that can be explored throughout the entire season. Given the vastness of the area, it is best for a newcomer to utilize the services of an experienced local guide before venturing out on one's own.

Seagirt Access

This city owned location offers access to beach and jetty fishing. Its proximity to the waters of the Atlantic makes it a potentially good location to fish in season.

Rockaway Beach

This expansive stretch of public beach is ocean-facing and, as such, receives good runs of fish during the spring and summer months. It is a very popular bathing beach, so early and late season fishing provides the best conditions and least congestion.

Bayswater Point State Park

This area provides for marsh shoreline fishing. Its location puts the park on the fringes of Jamaica Bay.

Conch Basin

This is another city facility with sandy beach and marshy shoreline access to Rockaway Community Park.

Dubos Point Wildlife Sanctuary

Good location on the fringes of Jamaica Bay that offers marshy shoreline and rocky beach access.

Brant Point Wildlife Sanctuary

A well-positioned city-owned sanctuary providing for marshy shoreline and rocky beach access. It too rests on the fringes of Jamaica Bay.

Jacob Riis Park

This is a National Park Service area with beach access fronting the Atlantic Ocean. Its location affords some potentially excellent fishing conditions during seasonal movements of gamefish.

Fort Tilden

Moving down the Rockaway peninsula is Fort Tilden, another National Park Service property. This area offers beach and jetty fishing access.

Rockaway Point

This well-situated National Park Service area lies at the tip of the peninsula and can offer potentially outstanding beach and jetty fishing. Access is available twenty-four hours a day with a valid permit.

Broad Channel Park

This is a city park with marshy shorelines and a sandy beach.

Joseph P. Addabo Bridge

This access is provided through the National Park Service. Fishing is from sandy and rocky beaches around the area of the bridge.

Queens North

The northern sections of Queens allow the fly angler access to some very diverse fishing situations. Following an almost a semi-circular route at the northernmost tip of the borough, an angler can begin at the old Worlds Fair Marina and work around through Flushing Bay, then the upper reaches of the East River into the lower parts of the Long Island Sound and Little Neck Bay. This last area in particular is a very productive early-season area for striped bass. It is bordered by Queens on one side and a small slice of Nassau County on the other. Year in and year out, many of the earliest reports of stripers come from the waters of Little Neck Bay. It is a perennial favorite of fly anglers and produces fine numbers of school-sized fish. When bigger baits are present, it also relinquishes its fair share of large stripers. Once the waters of the bay warm to summer levels, the fishing slows. The lower parts of the Long Island Sound off Queens are also excellent early-season waters for the boating angler, but fish will remain in the lower Sound throughout most of the season. Bass, some weakfish, bluefish, and the occasional bonito or false albacore make up the bulk of the fly angler's fishery. All of the access points in this area are New York City-owned.

Herman A. MacNeil Park

Primarily bulkhead and steep shoreline fishing at this New York City Park. The park extends out into an area bordered by the upper reaches of the East River and Flushing Bay.

Powell's Cove Park

Located inside of Powell's Cove, this park offers access to a rocky beach and a marshy shoreline.

Francis Lewis Park

Located in the vicinity of the Whitestone Bridge, this city park allows access to a sandy stretch of beach.

Little Bay Park and Fort Totten

Located inside of Little Bay, both rocky beach and jetty fishing can be accessed. Both locations provide for some surprisingly good, early striped bass fishing.

Bayside Marina/Crocheron Park

Located in Little Neck Bay, this marina offers a hard-surface launching facility as well as pier and shoreline fishing.

Queens West

Most of these locations offer access to portions of the East River and Roosevelt Island. Much of this fishing is from a pier and bulkhead, but a number of areas do offer access to beaches and shoreline fishing. Almost all are New York City-owned access points. The locations are: Grand Ferry Park (shoreline/beach); Queensbridge Park (bulkhead); Rainey Park (bulkhead); Socrates Sculpture Park (steep shoreline); Hallets Cove (bulkhead); Ralph DeMarco Park (steep shoreline).

New Jersey

The Garden State is recognized as having the highest population density of any state in the United States. New Jersey also has a substantial amount of ocean-facing coastline relative to its size that totals 130 miles. In addition, the entire New Jersey tidal shoreline is calculated at 1,792 miles, providing plenty of surf and wade fishing opportunities for flyfishing surf anglers. There are also numerous locations throughout the state that offer access to beaches, jetties, backwater bank fishing, bulkheads, and sea walls. Some of the those locations provide better flyfishing opportunities than others, but all offer access where an angler can cast a fly line and have a chance at tangling with premier inshore gamefish.

The Atlantic Ocean runs a course that parallels almost the entire length of the state with many public beaches dotting the coastline. Major bays like Barnegat, Raritan, and Delaware provide countless flyfishing scenarios, as do the smaller back bays scattered about the interior of the state. Numerous state parks and wildlife management areas provide a wealth of access points for saltwater fly fishing that range from remote areas of the state to metropolitan areas. New Jersey also offers significant number of tidal access points to some excellent bank and bulkhead fishing. While these latter two may not always be ideal for fly fishing, these situations are worth exploring throughout the season.

The New Jersey sand beaches are some of the finest throughout the region, with several iconic stretches of sand like that which is part of Island Beach State Park. The quality of fishing along the Jersey Shore has increased dramatically since the resurgence of striped bass activity of the 1990s. Both spring and fall runs of bass along New Jersey's coastline can be as good as surf fishing gets. Recent years have also seen those bass linger along these beaches, especially when large concentrations of menhaden or sand eels have been present. In past seasons, striped bass remained in these water well into the winter months before heading farther south. Most of this action occurs along the Jersey beaches, creating ideal opportunities for the wading fly angler. Beaches, bays, backcountry, and tidal rivers define the complete scope of what New Jersey has to offer saltwater anglers.

BAYS

There are literally dozens of locations in New Jersey that can be classified as bays, coves, and backwaters. All such formations offer numerous prospects for the fly angler. Striped bass, especially, will frequent these areas and remain throughout the seasons. Bluefish, weakfish, fluke, and occasionally small pelagics are seen. There is plenty of territory to be explored.

Delaware Bay is a major body of water rimmed by New Jersey and Delaware. It is an estuary into which the Delaware River flows. The Bay covers almost 782 square miles and is a mix of tidal mud flats and salt marshes. The bay is a place where salt water and fresh water merge, an exciting confluence that attracts all sorts of bait and gamefish. It is a nurturing ground and nursery for many species of fish and wildlife. In addition to the Delaware River, a number of others New Jersey streams and rivers flow into the bay: Cohansey River; Maurice River; and the Salem River. Some very large striped bass come from the waters of Delaware Bay each spring, especially bass that are hot on the heels of migrating herring and shad.

Larger and popular bays with suitable access are as follows: Absecon Bay, Atlantic County; Barnegat Bay, Ocean County; Great Egg Harbor Bay, Cape May

County; Little Bay, Atlantic County; Manahawkin Bay, Ocean County; Raritan Bay, Monmouth County; Sandy Hook Bay; Monmouth County; and Tuckerton Bay, Ocean County.

Some of the secondary bays that are good fishing holes include: Basses Bay, Ocean County; Blackberry Bay, Monmouth County; Carnival Bay, Cape May County; Eagle Bay, Atlantic County; Genesis Bay, Cape May County; Grassy Bay, Atlantic County; Great Bay, Atlantic County; Great Swan Bay, Ocean County; Lakes Bay, Atlantic County; Lower Bay, Monmouth County; Ludlam Bay, Cape May County; Mankiller Bay, Atlantic County; Oyster Bay, Monmouth County; Paradise Bay, Cape May County; Peck Bay, Cape May County; Reeds Bay, Atlantic County; Sanctuary Bay, Cape May County; Skull Bay, Atlantic County; Shelter Island Bay, Atlantic County; Somers Bay, Atlantic County; and Strathmere Bay, Cape May County.

PARKS

New Jersey municipal and state parks offer wonderful opportunities to fish the state's beaches, harbors, bays, and backwaters. With one of the most extensive coastlines in the Northeast and plenty of backcountry landscapes, the Garden State is one of the finest wade fishing destinations along the entire length of the East Coast. Numerous parks provide access to that fishing and offer other amenities which make for an enjoyable angling experience.

One of the most storied stretches of surf-fishing beach is contained within Island Beach State Park (IBSP). This area sees both magnificent spring and fall runs for striped bass and bluefish, as well as a late season influx of false albacore. IBSP is a barrier island that extends almost ten miles along the Atlantic Ocean and Barnegat Bay. The southern extremity of the park borders Barnegat Inlet. Aside from being a natural wonderland, this piece of real estate is one of the most productive surf-fishing locations along the Northeast and mid-Atlantic coasts. This location hosts one of the finest spring and fall runs of striped bass in the region.

Other New Jersey parks worth exploring include: Liberty State Park, Jersey City; Sadowski Park, Perth Amboy; Old Bridge Waterfront Park, Laurence Harbor; Aberdeen Municipal Park; Keyport Marine Park; Union Beach Municipal Park; Highlands Marine Park; Hartshorne Woods Park, Middletown; Municipal Marine Park, Red Bank; Shark River County Park, Neptune; Gull Island County Park, Point Pleasant; Island Beach State Park; Cattus Island County Park, Toms River; Riverfront Landing County Park, Toms River; Mill Creek County Park, Berkley Township; Barnegat Lighthouse State Park; South Green Street County Park, Tuckerton; Corson's Inlet State Park, Cape May; Townsend Inlet Waterfront Park, Cape May; Bayfront Municipal Park, Cape May; Cape May Point State Park; and Leesburg Municipal River Park.

WILDLIFE MANAGEMENT AREAS

These locations are generally multipurpose recreational areas that offer visitors more than just a fishing experience. Generally, all are great places to observe marine life and wildlife, when not angling for gamefish species.

One of the most impressive of the region's areas is the Gateway National Recreation Area. Although mostly concentrated in New York State, and with eleven specific park tracts, the Sandy Hook Unit is unique to New Jersey. This segment of the park is located in Monmouth County and is classified as a barrier peninsula. Sites within the park that provide access for anglers are Fort Hancock and the branches of Sandy Hook. In addition to beaches, the area's landscape and seascape is also comprised of salt marshes and marine forest.

New Jersey's other WMA with coastal or tidal access include: Point Pleasant Canal Wildlife Management Area; Metedeconk River County Conservation Area; Edwin B. Forsythe National Wildlife Refuge; Manahawkin Wildlife Management Area; Great Bay Boulevard Wildlife Management Area, Tuckerton; Green Bank-Swan Bay Wildlife Management Area, Burlington; Port Republic Wildlife Management Area; Absecon Wildlife Management Area; Pork Island Wildlife Management Area, Egg Harbor; MacNamara Wildlife Management Area, Egg Harbor; Tuckahoe Wildlife Management Area, Cape May; Beesley Point Wildlife Management Area, Cape May; Higby Beach Wildlife Management Area; Dennis Creek Wildlife Management Area; Millville Wildlife Management Area; Heislerville Wildlife Management Area; Egg Island Wildlife Management Area; Fortesque Wildlife Management Area; Nantuxent Wildlife Management Area, Newport; New Sweede Wildlife Management Area, Bay Point; Dix Wildlife Management Area, Sea Breeze; Gum Tree Corner Wildlife Management Area, Stowe Creek; and Mad Horse Creek Wildlife Management Area, Canton.

BEACHES

New Jersey enjoys a wealth of ocean-facing beaches to explore along its extensive Atlantic coastline. These locations are all suitable for anglers wading for striped bass, bluefish, summer flounder, and false albacore. Beaches run almost the entire length of the state, north to south, and most stops will yield fish in season. Gamefish opportunities are common throughout the range of New Jersey beaches and the seasons typically progress south to north up the coast, with beaches around Cape May turning on first early in the spring, followed in progression as beaches farther up the coast literally heat up. Most New Jersey beach access is provided at the municipal level, so local access ordinances should be checked.

The following are some places to wet a fly line when you are in the neighborhood: Bloomers Beach, Bergen County; Monmouth Beach, Long Branch; Seven President's Beach, Long Branch; Deal Municipal Beach; Allenhurst Municipal Beach; Asbury Park Municipal Beach; Ocean Grove Municipal Beach; Bradley Beach Municipal Beach; Avon By The Sea Municipal Beach; Belmar Municipal Beach; Spring Lake Municipal Beach; Sea Girt Municipal Bach; Manasquan Municipal Beach; Point Pleasant Beach; Maxon Avenue Beach, Point Pleasant; Bay Head Municipal Beach; Brickton Municipal Beach; Mantoloking Municipal Beach; Normandy Beach Municipal Beach; Lavalette Municipal Beach; Ortley Beach Municipal Beach; Seaside Heights Municipal Beach; Barnegat Light Municipal Beach; Loveladies Municipal Beach; Long Beach Township Municipal Beach; Surf City Municipal Beach; Ship Bottom Municipal Beach; Brant Beach Municipal Beach; Brighton Beach Municipal Beach; Peahala Park Municipal Beach; Spray Beach Municipal Beach; Beachhaven Municipal Beach; Holgate Municipal Beach; Brigantine Municipal Beach; Atlantic City Municipal Beach; Ventnor Municipal Beach; Margate Municipal Beach; Longport Municipal Beach; Ocean City Municipal Beach; Strathmore Municipal Beach; Sea Isle City Municipal Beach; Avalon Municipal Beach; Stone Harbor Municipal Beach; Wildwood Municipal Beach; Cape May City Municipal Beach; Sunset Beach, Lower Township; Kimples Beach, Middle Township; Cooks Beach, Middle Township; Reeds Beach, Middle Township; Gandy's Beach, Downe.

Delaware and Maryland

The mid-Atlantic states of Delaware and Maryland enjoy a combined coastline of approximately sixty miles and a total tidal shoreline of about 3,571 miles. Much of this tidal span is attributed to the widespread watershed of the Chesapeake Bay and its tributaries, a hallmark fishery within this region, and Delaware Bay that hosts as diverse a fishery as can be found anywhere throughout the mid-Atlantic states. Both states enjoy very productive fly fishing in back bays as well as from sand beaches that face the Atlantic Ocean. Fishing in this region offers something of a transition from Northeast to Southeast, in that you can catch a blend of species from both regions, for example, striped bass, bluefish, puppy drum, and spotted seatrout.

DELAWARE

Port Mahon

Port Mahon sits on the shore of Delaware Bay and offers access to a number of bay fishing areas including Port Mahon Preserve and the Port Mahon River.

Bennett's Pier, Beach

This location is a popular surf-fishing destination on Delaware Bay.

Beach Plum Island Reserve

Located across in Lewes, Delaware, is Beach Plum Island Preserve. It is part of the Cape Henlopen State Park. The reserve is one of the last undeveloped barrier islands in Delaware and offers state access to fishing areas. Delaware Bay and the Broadkill River border the reserve.

Cape Henlopen State Park

This state park is located in Lewes, Delaware and provides access to sand beaches suitable for surf fishing. The area also contains tidal mud flats that hold fish. The Herring Point section of the park contains groins that function as fish-attracting structures. Motor vehicle access to the shoreline is achieved through three points of entry: the Point Crossing; the Navy Crossing; and Gordons Pond.

Broadkill Beach

Broadkill Beach provides surf fishing access to the Delaware Bay. The beach is in proximity to the Prime Hook National Wildlife Refuge and also borders Beach Plum Island State Park.

Broadkill River

The Broadkill River is located in Sussex County and flows into Delaware Bay. The river is in proximity to the Cedar Creek watershed, Rehoboth Bay, and the Indian River watershed.

Lewes Beach

Lewes, Delaware is ideally located where Delaware Bay and the Atlantic Ocean join. Lewes Beach is a popular surf-fishing destination in this area.

Canary Creek

The mouth of Canary Creek and the adjacent marsh offer fine opportunities for fly fishing. The creek is located in Sussex County.

Indian River Inlet

This area offers access to both shoreline fishing as well as jetty fishing on the north and south sides of the inlet. Areas like the North Pocket, the Causeway Pipes, and the backside rocks also offer other angling opportunities.

Delaware Seashore State Park

Bordered by the Indian River Bay, Rehoboth Bay, and the Atlantic Ocean, this location is one of the best surf-fishing areas in the state. The barrier island is blessed with sand beaches, salt marshes, islands, shallows, and jetties, all of which will hold fish at different times of the season. Other access points within the park include: the two Towers Road segments (offering shoreline access to both Rehoboth Bay and the Atlantic Ocean) and 3 R's Road.

Fenwick Island State Park

This popular and relatively pristine state park sits between Fenwick Island, Ocean City, and Bethany Beach. The beaches of the park are the big draw for surf anglers. The park allows permitted beach vehicles and offers beach access via three designated dune crossings.

MARYLAND

Ocean City Beaches

The approximately ten-mile stretch of Ocean City Beaches offers public access to numerous surf-fishing locations. Liberal numbers of access points make these beaches ideal for the visiting fly angler. In addition to the ocean-facing sand beaches, the Ocean City North jetty is another top angling spot, as are the areas around the Ocean City Inlet and the Ocean Pier. Stinky Beach is another surf-fishing location in Ocean City.

Assateague Island National Seashore

The beaches of Assateague Island are host to some of the best inshore and surf fly fishing along the mid-Atlantic coast. Assateague Island is blessed with beaches, inlets, back bays, tidal creeks, and surf. The area is noted for its abundance of game-fish species, including striped bass, bluefish, red drum, summer flounder, spotted seatrout, and croaker.

Chesapeake Bay

The Chesapeake Bay has the distinction of being the largest estuary in the Unites States. Its upper, middle, and lower sections offer numerous flyfishing op-portunities, including many wade fishing scenarios. The bay encompasses almost 200 miles and extends from the Susquehanna River to the Atlantic Ocean. The total shoreline that defines the bay is approximately 11,600 miles. Some of the more popu-lar areas of interest to fly anglers fishing areas in the bay are: Sandy Point State Park, the Susquehanna Flats, North Beach, the area around the Chesapeake Bay Bridge-Tunnel, Mid-Point Beach, and South Point.

Virginia

The state of Virginia enjoys a coastline that stretches approximately 112 miles and a total tidal shoreline that encompasses 3,315 miles, offering many diverse opportunities for the surf and wading fly angler. Virginia represents somewhat of a melting pot of species that converge upon this location, while migrating or remaining in residence throughout the seasons. Fish species from the Southeast mingle with gamefish from the Northeast, so it is not unusual to catch striped bass, red drum, bluefish, seatrout, summer flounder, and croaker. Virginia also shares the Chesapeake Bay with Maryland. Three of the most emblematic saltwater surf-fishing spots in Virginia are Virginia Beach, the Eastern Shore of Virginia, and the Assateague Island National Seashore.

EASTERN SHORE

This seventy-mile long region of Virginia offers a wealth of flyfishing opportunities along the Atlantic Ocean shoreline. It is part of the Delmarva Peninsula, and has a long tradition of fishing-related activities. The Eastern Shore lies apart from the rest of Virginia, separated by the Chesapeake Bay. The configuration of the "shore" includes a number of barrier islands, all of which offer flyfishing opportunities: Chincoteague Island is situated along the north-end Atlantic side of the shore, while the southern portion of pristine Assateague Island National Seashore is in Virginia and includes Chincoteague National Wildlife Refuge. The area also has many back bays, coves, and marshes, all suitable for fly fishing.

Chesapeake Bay Bridge-Tunnel

The area around the CBBT is well known for large striped bass. Areas adjacent to and contiguous with the span offer flyfishing opportunities, especially locations near the manmade islands that support the entire structure. The CBBT spans approximately twenty-three miles and connects the Eastern Shore to Virginia Beach and the remainder of the state.

Rudee Inlet

While the harbor inside of Rudee Inlet is home to a fleet of large sporting vessels, the beaches and jetties on either side of the inlet offer access to the wading fly angler and a wealth of varied gamefish species.

Lynnhaven Inlet

This inlet connects to the Atlantic Ocean and is adjacent to the terminal point of the Lynnhaven River where it empties into the Chesapeake Bay. Lynnhaven Inlet is situated at the north end of Virginia Beach. The area is a popular inshore fishing destination known for the quality of its striped bass, bluefish, and summer flounder fisheries.

Virginia Beach

The entire length of Virginia Beach has a well-earned reputation as a surf fisherman's paradise. Many indigenous species of gamefish prowl the surf line while others migrate up and down the coastline. Seasonally, a number of varied inshore sport fish can be caught. These include: black drum, red drum, bluefish, croaker, summer flounder, sea bass, speckled trout, tautog, cobia, Spanish mackerel, striped bass, and grey trout. Under the right conditions, all can be caught on flies.

Cape Charles

The town of Cape Charles includes two public beaches on the Eastern Shore. Both beaches are excellent for surf fishing. The area around the town fishing pier is also worth prospecting with flies.

Kiptopeke State Park

The park is located on the Eastern Shore and offers access to coastal habitats of the Chesapeake bay. The waterfront and the beaches offer fine surf fishing, especially the southernmost beach. The fishing pier is also accessible twenty-four hours a day, and lights around the area attract many species of fish at night.

First Landing State Park

The almost 3,000-acre park is situated at Cape Henry in North Virginia Beach. It contains one and a quarter miles of beach along the shoreline of Chesapeake Bay. Access to the beach is available every day of the year.

Back Bay National Wildlife Refuge

This refuge encompasses more than 9,000 acres and is situated in Virginia Beach. Although much of Back Bay National Wildlife Refuge is a freshwater ecosystem, the refuge lies between the Atlantic Ocean and Currituck Sound. The character of the refuge is defined by a number of barrier islands that offer ocean beach and marsh access. No vehicular traffic is permitted so access is via foot or bicycle.

False Cape State Park

The park abuts the Back Bay Wildlife Refuge. It is part of a barrier island that sits between Back Bay and the Atlantic Ocean. The coastline of the park provides ample opportunities for fishing. As a primitive coastal ecosystem, access to False

Cape State Park is gained by boat, on foot, or via bicycle. Due to both the saline and brackish composition of the water surrounding the park, a variety of gamefish species can be caught, predominant among those being summer flounder, red drum, and croaker.

Rivers

The tidal sections of rivers like the James River, the Rappahannock River, and the Potomac River are productive places to wet a fly line. Chippokes Plantation State Park has almost two miles of beach on the James River that is ideal for shoreline fishing. The Northern Neck region contains several Potomac River beaches, including Colonial Beach and the beach at Westmoreland State Park. The Rappahannock River is one of the finest fishing destinations in the state of Virginia. The lower section of river represents a blend of freshwater, brackish-water, and saltwater angling. In addition to freshwater gamefish, several anadromous species like striped bass, American shad, and herring migrate up and down the river and its tributaries and offer fine flyfishing scenarios.

North and South Carolina

The Carolinas enjoy a combined coastline of 488 miles and a total tidal shoreline of approximately 6,200 miles. Along with that volume of marine real estate comes an abundance of saltwater flyfishing opportunities. Ocean-facing beaches, barrier islands, sand flats, backcountry habitat, salt marshes, inlets, grass flats, and sounds are all part of the flyfishing options available throughout the Carolinas. Both states are also blessed with some of the best diversity of gamefish species along the entire East Coast: croaker, black drum, bluefish, bonito, cobia, pompano, flounder, little tunny, red drum, sheepshead, barracuda, Spanish mackerel, jacks, spotted seatrout, weakfish, and striped bass. The region also contains some of the most well-recognized saltwater flyfishing destinations in the country, like North Carolina's legendary Outer Banks and the South Carolina Lowcountry's Hilton Head.

NORTH CAROLINA

The Tar Heel state offers the saltwater fly angler many opportunities for excellent fishing. According to Captain Gordon Churchill, one of the region's most accomplished flyfishing guides, "There are may good spots for fly rodders, all with fine current and areas with moderate waves. Many can be reached by car and kayak, while some will need a boat to gain wade access. And others still can be accessed by ferry." All in all, there are many alternatives for access.

Oregon Inlet

The beaches adjacent to the inlet are renowned for the quality of surf fishing, especially in the fall and during the month of November. Striped bass, bluefish, albies, puppy drum, trout, and croaker are all within reach of the surf fly angler.

Pea Island

Pea Island is located at the tip of Hatteras Island and contains the Pea Island National Wildlife Refuge. The Pea Island Slough is considered one of the area's better locations for fly fishing, especially for reds and seatrout.

Propeller Slough

The slough is located east of the Oregon Inlet Fishing Center. The channel extends a few hundred yards and provides an excellent wading opportunity. Shallow, with moving water, the slough attracts speckled trout, bluefish, redfish, flounder, Spanish mackerel, croaker, and striped bass.

Cape Lookout

Cape Lookout National Seashore is a true natural gem. The pristine and remote islands and beaches of the Cape offer some of the finest fly fishing in the region for a multitude of gamefish, especially for false albacore in the fall. Some of the largest concentration of big albies typically swarm around Harkers Island in November. The area channels around the Harkers Island Bridge are an excellent trout location. The islands of the Cape are accessible by boat and ferry service.

Cape Hatteras

The entirety of Cape Hatteras is a surf angler's wonderland, with beaches that offer fly opportunities that are as good they get. Leading the way are big bull redfish, but many other abundant gamefish species are little tunny, Spanish mackerel, striped bass, flounder, bluefish, pompano, and spotted seatrout. The area provides a range of angling scenarios, from surf casting from ocean-facing beaches to backwater areas and shallow water flats.

Beaufort Inlet

The area in and around the inlet is well known for the fall run of false albacore, but it also hosts a fine fishery for spotted seatrout, Spanish mackerel, and bluefish.

Fort Macon State Park

The park rests within a barrier island situated between Beaufort and Morehead City. While the beaches in proximity to the park offer quality surf fishing, one of the main attractions of this location are the rock jetties that form the inlet that connects backwaters to the Atlantic Ocean. The inlet jetties attract all forms of migrating gamefish, including striped bass, bluefish, seatrout, summer flounder, Spanish mackerel, and gray trout.

Cedar Island

The community of Cedar Island is steeped in a long tradition of fishing. The island contains miles of unspoiled beaches and marshes. The area is also home to the Cedar Island Wildlife Refuge and is in proximity to Cedar Island Bay, Core Island and Pamlico Sound. The sloughs and flats around the ferry launch are also productive spots to fish.

Bogue Inlet

Located in Emerald Isle, the inlet and adjacent beaches offer access to quality fishing for bluefish, flounder, sheepshead, Spanish mackerel, black drum, pompano, and grey trout, as well as other migratory species.

Masonboro Island

Accessible by boat or kayak, this is on of the largest undeveloped barrier islands in North Carolina. The island sits between the Atlantic Ocean and the Intracoastal Waterway. The flats on the sound side of the island as well as the open beach and jetty are good places to wade fish. Most local gamefish species are willing to eat flies.

Fort Fisher

The Fort Fisher State Recreation Area is a multi-use destination that offers access to approximately six miles of unspoiled sand beaches. It is located near Wilmington and lies between the Atlantic Ocean and the Cape Fear River. In addition to ocean-facing beaches, the recreation area also contains extensive salt marshes, sand, and mud flats and tidal creeks, all of which attract and hold a myriad of gamefish.

Cape Fear

The entire shoreline of Cape Fear offers fly anglers access to exceptional surf and wade fishing opportunities. The cape protrudes into the Atlantic Ocean from Bald Head Island and is comprised of barrier beaches, sand dunes, and a variety of beach- and seagrasses. The pristine skinny water is ideal for sight casting, primarily to redfish. Bluefish, seatrout, flounder, and croaker are also available. The Cape Fear estuary is also a fertile fishery. Currents in this region can be severe and dangerous, as evidenced by the moniker, "Graveyard of the Atlantic."

Pamlico Sound

Pamlico Sound is a large lagoon that extends from Oregon Inlet to Drum Inlet. It is the largest lagoon on the East Coast and its waters contain a myriad of gamefish species: Striped bass (rockfish), flounder, red and puppy drum, speckled trout, and Spanish mackerel.

Beaufort Inlet

Beaufort Inlet is a deep water location through which large volumes of water move during tidal changes. The area in and around the inlet is host to plentiful numbers of gamefish. The Shackleford Bank area is another productive location.

SOUTH CAROLINA

The "Lowcountry" is a piece of South Carolina coastal real estate that extends from Georgetown to Beaufort counties. The area is rich in habitat that is conducive to healthy fisheries. Almost 2,900 miles of tidal coastline embrace estuaries, beaches, marshes, flats, and harbors that provide numerous opportunities for the wading fly angler.

Edisto Island Beach State Park

This 1,255-acre park is located on Edisto Island and contains access to one and a half miles of sand beach and salt marshes. The area is a popular surf-fishing destination and is suitable for fly fishing.

Hunting Island State Park

Hunting Island is located bear Beaufort. It is a remote barrier island where fishing is a popular pastime. The park offers a mix of surf, lagoon, and pier fishing. The area around the adjacent Fripp Inlet is also productive. Local gamefish suitable to target with the fly rod are redfish, seatrout, and croaker.

Huntington Beach State Park

This ocean front park is located in Murrells Inlet and contains a mixture ocean-facing sand beach, a lagoon, a salt marsh, and a maritime forest. With three miles of pristine beach to walk and wade there are plenty of surf-fishing opportunities within this park. Fishing can be excellent for seatrout, red drum, flounder, sheepshead, black drum, pompano, Spanish macks, and jack crevalle.

Myrtle Beach

Saltwater fishing and Myrtle Beach go hand in hand. The area has direct access to the ocean-facing beaches of the Atlantic Ocean; backcountry access via the Intracoastal Waterway; marshes, tidal rivers, and creeks; and Myrtle Beach State Park that contains one mile of beach. Redfish, seatrout, and flounder are high on the chart of species that are targeted by surf fly anglers.

Hilton Head

Hilton Head Island offers access to a variety of wade-fishing scenarios: Atlantic Ocean beaches, sound shoreline, brackish water, tidal lagoons, and tidal creeks. All beaches on Hilton Head Island are open to the public. The beaches and the lagoon network attract and hold redfish, black drum, flounder, striped bass, bluefish, and tarpon.

Kiawah Island

This barrier island is situated near Charleston and attracts a variety of gamefish, most notably, redfish, spotted seatrout, and flounder. The Island is also known for its largemouth bass ponds. Brackish water, beach front, tidal creeks, and river mouths are all ideal places to wade with fly rod in hand.

Other Beach Locations

The following locations offer access to a variety of venues for fly fishing: beaches, salt marshes, and tidal creeks. Pawleys Island, located south of Myrtle Beach, has four miles of beach and a network of tidal marshes; Litchfield Beach, also near Myrtle Beach, has miles of ocean-facing sand beaches; Surfside Beach boasts two miles of ocean beach with thirty-six access points; Bull Island has some secluded beaches that are part of the Cape Romaine National Wildlife Refuge.

Folly Beach is a seven-mile-long stretch of sand located close to the city of Charleston; Isle of Palms contains seven miles of sand beaches; Seabrook Island offers access to a unspoiled sand beaches on the Atlantic Ocean and the shores of the Edisto River, as well as and salt marshes and tidal creeks; and Fripp Island, near Beaufort, offers private access to almost three and a half miles of sand beach.

Georgia

The Peach State boasts 100 miles of coastline, 2,344 miles of tidal shoreline, and a network of remote barrier islands that offer myriad opportunities for wade fishing. The region also contains areas of backcountry, salt marshes, and tidal creeks that attract numerous varieties of gamefish indigenous to the Southeast. Some of the state's best fishing can be found on and along the network of barrier islands, including those of the Golden Isles. Although those islands contain a significant amount of private property, public access to barrier island beaches is allowed to the high tide line. When in doubt about such access, check local ordinances.

Wilmington Island

Located on Georgia's east coast, Wilmington Island is a popular shore fishing destination. The Island is detached from the mainland and adjacent to Wassaw Sound. The south side of the island tends to attract the most anglers seeking to fly fish the area, with spotted seatrout, flounder, and redfish. Tidal creeks and ponds, salt marshes, and beaches make for the ideal fish habitat.

Tybee Island

Tybee Island is situated approximately eighteen miles from Savannah and is one of the most accessible of the islands. Savannah Beach is one of the more popular surf-fishing locations on the island for red and black drum and spotted seatrout. In addition to beach front fishing on Tybee Island, areas around rock jetties, oyster beds, marshes, piers, and bridges will also attract and hold gamefish.

Wassaw Island

Wassaw Island is also located near Savannah. The island is approximately fourteen miles south of the city. Wassaw Island is considered by many to be one of Georgia's most pristine islands. The island is home to the Wassaw National Wildlife Refuge, accessible via water. This multi-use refuge offers access for surf fishing. In addition to seven miles of remote ocean-facing beaches the island and surrounding area also contains salt marshes, mud and sand flats, and tidal creeks, all habitats conducive to supporting healthy fisheries.

St. Catherines Island

Although St. Catherines Island is privately owned, it is worth mentioning since riparian rights allow angler access below the mean high tide mark. Water access via boat or kayak can provide opportunities for the wading angler. St. Catherines is approximately ten miles long and is positioned between St. Catherines Sound and Sapelo Sound. In addition to the beaches, St. Catherines contains a significant amount of wetlands, salt marshes, and tidal backcountry areas.

Little St. Simons Island

The greatest appeal of Little St. Simons Island is its unspoiled natural character. Seven miles of undisturbed beaches are a hallmark of the island, as are numerous tidal creeks that attract and hold fish. The island is bracketed by the Hampton River,

Buttermilk Sound, and St. Simons Island. Spotted seatrout, redfish, black drum, and flounder are plentiful and primary targets for fly anglers.

St. Simons Island

St. Simons Island is a fishing jewel of the Golden Isles. It is a popular destination for both offshore and inshore anglers. The island provides access to a wide array of fishing opportunities, including sand beaches, tidal creeks, rivers, and salt marshes. The primary quarry available to the wading angler are redfish, spotted seatrout, and flounder, along with the occasional nearshore tarpon.

Jeykll Island

This popular fishing destination is also a part of the Golden Isles chain and includes several miles of ocean-facing sand beaches suitable for wade fishing. The north end of the island is the most unspoiled. The island offers excellent fishing for spotted seatrout and redfish.

Cumberland Island

This is one of the longest islands in the Golden Isles chain at almost eighteen miles tip to tip. The island is located along Georgia's southern coast. In addition to oceanside beaches, Cumberland Island contains a wealth of salt marshes, tidal creeks, and mud and sand flats. Dungeness Beach is a popular location for anglers wading the shore.

Florida

The Sunshine State is our last but certainly not least flyfishing destination along the East Coast. Florida anglers have been chasing saltwater gamefish with the fly rod longer than most any other segment of the flyfishing community. This tendency is with good reason. There are areas along Florida's Atlantic Ocean coastline (the east coast) and the shores of the Gulf of Mexico (the west coast) that offer countless surf-fishing opportunities. It would literally take a few lifetimes to explore all the beaches, bays, and backcountry that comprise Florida's east and west coasts. Aside from the fishing opportunities afforded the fly angler via boat and flats skiff, the wading possibilities are as close to limitless as they are along any areas of the East Coast. The predominant gamefish species can keep a fly angler engaged throughout an entire year. Throughout the year and during peak phases of the seasons, myriad species of gamefish can be caught in Florida, north to south and east to west. Some of the more predominant fish that can be caught from the surf and wading backwaters include: redfish, spotted seatrout, flounder, snook, sheepshead, jack crevalle, black drum, bluefish, tarpon, ladyfish, Spanish mackerel, pompano, bonefish, and permit. While Florida's ocean-facing sand beaches offer miles upon miles of contiguous surf-fishing opportunities, Florida's backcountry is world renowned for seemingly endless expanses of remote and wild areas; and the Florida Keys are a fishing world unto themselves. Florida's coastal fishing destinations can be categorized as follows: Northeast Florida; Central Florida; South Florida; Florida Keys; South West Florida; and the Panhandle.

NORTHEAST FLORIDA COAST

The northeast Florida region is defined loosely as extending from the Florida/Georgia border, and in and around Jacksonville down to an area just north of Daytona Beach. The region includes Amelia Island, the last in a chain of Sea Islands that extends from South Carolina to Florida. Located off the Jacksonville coast, Amelia Island is approximately thirteen miles long and four miles wide and is an excellent location for redfish, spotted seatrout, and jacks.

Within the range of the Florida's northeast coast are a wealth of surf- and wade-fishing opportunities, from beaches and tidal marshes to state parks and national wildlife management areas. Some of the areas worth prospecting with the fly rod include: Atlantic Beach; Jacksonville Beach; Fernandina Beach; Ponte Vedra Beach; GMT National Estuarine area; South Ponte Vedra Beach; Villano Beach; St. Augustine Beach; Butler Beach; Crescent Beach; Fort Matanzas; Summer Haven; the beaches of Palm Coast that extend for almost nineteen miles; Beverly Beach; and Flagler Beach.

Big Talbot and Little Talbot Islands can also be explored. Once down around the St. Augustine area, Anastasia Island also allows fishing. Guana River State Park contains two beaches and almost 2,400 acres of estuary, tidal marsh, and preserve.

CENTRAL FLORIDA COAST

Central Florida is typically identified as representing a broad section of real estate located in the center of the state that embraces the interior, the Gulf Coast, and the central east coast of the state. The coastal stretch within this region runs from about Daytona Beach to Stuart and Fort Pierce, Florida. On the Gulf Coast side, the central region extends from the area known as the Big Bend (where the coastline turns into the Panhandle) down to about Tampa Bay. The region also includes the Indian and Mosquito Lagoons and the entirety of the Space Coast, which offer some of the finest fly fishing in the state for redfish, seatrout, and black drum. Kay Biscayne is also part of this geographic area. While not one of the true Florida Keys, it is an island with many of the same characteristics of the Keys and hosts excellent shallow water fishing.

The following areas and beaches provide access and opportunity for fly anglers: Gamble Rogers Memorial State Recreation Area; North Peninsula State Recreation

Area; Tomoka State Park; Ormond Beach; Daytona Beach; Daytona Beach Shores; Ponce Inlet; Pons Park; Lighthouse Point Park; Smyrna Dunes Park; New Smyrna Beach; Canaveral National Seashore; Titusville; Merritt Island National Wildlife Refuge; Indian River Lagoon; Cocoa Beach; Orlando Beach; Satellite Beach; Indian Harbor Beach; Melbourne Beach; Sebastian Inlet; Wabasso Beach; Vero Beach; Avalon State Park; Jack Island Preserve State Park; Fort Pierce Inlet State Park; Savannas Recreation Area and State Park; Jensen Beach; St. Lucie Inlet Preserve State Park; Stuart; and Hobe Sound.

SOUTH FLORIDA COAST

The south Florida coast is loosely defined as including the southernmost part of the peninsula. It typically is described as including Miami-Dade, Broward, and Palm Beach counties. For purposes of demographic statistics, this part of Florida often includes the Keys and the southern end of Collier County on the west coast, but for purposes of flyfishing opportunities, the Keys and southwest Florida are treated separately. A unique feature of the south Florida coast is that it has a tropical climate where a mean temperature of sixty-four degrees or above is maintained throughout all twelve months of the year. This is the only such tropical climate in the United States. The benefit of this climate upon fishing is that tropical temperatures are conducive to supporting strong populations of gamefish like bonefish, permit, tarpon, and snook.

South Florida coastal surf-fishing areas and beaches include: Jupiter; Juno Beach; North Palm Beach; Riviera Beach; West Palm Beach; Boynton Beach; Delray Beach; Boca Raton; Deerfield Beach; Lighthouse Point; Pompano Beach; Fort Lauderdale; Dania Beach; North Miami Beach; Miami Beach; Biscayne Bay; and Biscayne National Park.

FLORIDA KEYS

While some definitions include the "Keys" in the South Florida region, the geology and fishing of the area are so distinct they need stand alone. The Keys are classified as a coral and limestone archipelago. They stretch from a point slightly below Miami south and west to Key West. The keys, or islands, extend along the Florida Straits and form a gentle boundary of Florida Bay, one of the most prolific saltwater fishing areas in the state. The Keys also offer the most varied flats fishing along the entire East Coast. There are five major keys, and all are of importance to the fly angler: Key Largo; Islamorada; Marathon; Big Pine Key and the Lower Keys; and Key West. All of the Keys are beneficiaries of a tropical climate. All the Keys enjoy superb fishing, and flyfishing opportunities abound. The wading fly angler will find numerous and quality surf, flats, and backcountry prospects for snook, bonefish, redfish, permit, and even tarpon in this region of the state.

Key Largo is referred to at the "first key," since it is the northernmost island in the chain. The key is positioned between the fish-attracting magnets that are the Everglades National Park and a coral barrier reef.

Islamorada is situated between Everglades National Park, a coral barrier reef, and the Florida Straits. Islamorada consists of six outlying islands: Plantation Key; Windley Key; Upper Matecumbe Key; Lower Matecumbe Key; Indian Key; and Lignumvitae Key. This area includes a wealth of shallow, backcountry fly fishing for snook, redfish, bonefish, permit, and tarpon. Islamorada has a well-earned reputation for being called the Sportfishing Capital of the World.

Marathon is a ten-mile-long island located in the middle of the Keys and it sits primarily on Fat Deer, Vaca, and Grassy Keys. This part of the Keys is deeply rooted in a generational tradition of fishing, and that applies to fly fishing as well.

Big Pine Key and the Lower Keys provide access to a network of great flyfishing locations that includes: Summerland Key, Big Torch and Little Torch Keys, Cudjoe Key, Sugarloaf Key; Big Coppitt; Ramrod Key; Little Duck Key; Ohio Key, the Saddlebunch Keys, and Bahia Honda State Park. This expanse of mangrove islands and lagoons is rich in flyfishing potential.

Key West is the land of Ernest Hemingway legends, Duval Street parades, great sunsets, and even greater fishing. Shallow flats, extensive mangrove islands, and wild backcountry are the backdrop for some of the most consistent and sustained year-round fishing.

SOUTHWEST FLORIDA COAST

This part of Florida lies along the southwest coast of the Gulf of Mexico. The coastal region typically includes an area south of Tampa Bay down to about Naples and Marco Island, and embraces Manatee, Sarasota, Charlotte, Lee, and Collier counties. The region contains some of the most pristine beaches in Florida. Among the most popular beaches and backcountry areas are those in and around Fort Myers, Sanibel, Captiva, Marco Island, Bonito Beach, Cape Coral, and Boca Grande.

Fort Myers contains twenty-five beaches on the Gulf side of Estero. Fort Myers Beach, the waters around Estero Island, Estero Bay and the State Park Preserve, San Carlos Bay, Lover's Key, and Bowdish Beach are all popular and productive areas to fly fish.

Bonita Beach also offers fine surf and wade opportunities at: Barefoot Beach Preserve County Park; Bonita Beach; Little Hickory Island Beach; Dog Beach; and the southern portion of Estero Bay.

Cape Coral contains hundreds of miles of canals, many of which are fishable from shore, bulkheads, and piers. The area also provides access to the Caloosahatchee River and the Gulf of Mexico. One of the most popular stretches of beach on Cape Coral is the Cape Coral Yacht Club Beach.

Sanibel Island is known as one of the best shelling destinations in the world, but its beaches and backwaters are equally renowned for the quality of the area's fishing. Some of the more popular places to fly fish include: Sanibel Island Beach; the Causeway Beaches; Lighthouse Beach; Tarpon Bay Beach; Bowman's Beach; Gulfside Park; Ding Darling National Wildlife Refuge; and the mangrove islands of Matlacha.

Captiva Island and its sister islands are the jewels of this region. I have enjoyed many wonderful days wading the gentle surf and backcountry that define this area. This is a great island to explore. Some destinations suitable for fly fishing are: Blind Pass; Alison Hagerup Beach; North Captiva; Captiva Pass; Safety Harbor; Useppa Island; Cabbage Key; Buck Key; Cayo Costa; Duck Key; Redfish Pass; and the South Seas Beach.

Boca Grande is known for its world-class run of large tarpon and the remarkable fishing for that species, which takes place in Boca Grande Pass. But equally notable is the inshore fishing for snook, seatrout, and redfish. Places to try are: Mexico Beach; Gasparilla Island Beach; and Boca Grande Beach. The area also contains fourteen remote walking paths that lead to beach access.

Marco Island hosts about six miles of beach and backwater that includes: Tigertail Beach; Marco Island Beach; Barfield Bay; Collier Bay; and Smokehouse Bay.

Naples beaches are among the most highly rated beaches in the Unites States, both for their natural beauty and for the fish that frequent the surf, flats, and backcountry. Some of the best places to wet a fly line are: Delnor Wiggins Pass State Recreation Area; Vanderbilt Beach; Calm Pass Beach; Lowdermilk Beach; and North Gulfshore Boulevard Beach.

THE FLORIDA PANHANDLE

This region of northwestern Florida is a stretch of the state that extends for about 227 miles along the Gulf of Mexico, from Pensacola to Apalachicola. This area is also referred to as the Emerald Coast because of is powdery white sand beaches and crystal-clear water. The quality of the area's fishing is as renowned as the beaches. A well-known Florida flyfishing captain once told me that the Panhandle is where other Florida guides come for their fishing vacations. That is quite an endorsement! Some of the beaches and towns that provide access for fishing are: Pensacola Beach; Grayton Beach; Panama City Beach; Port St. Joe; Fort Walton Beach; Apalachicola; Mexico Beach; St. George Island; Seagrove Beach; and Santa Rosa Beach.

Acknowledgments

While most of the information in this book has resulted from my personal fly fishing experiences, a project of this magnitude would not be possible without the input and support of many talented friends and colleagues. I would like to extend my sincerest thanks for the help, cooperation, and inspiration given me by the following individuals: Chris Paparo; FishGuyPhotos.com; Captain Rich Santos; flyfishjax.com; Captain Nick Angelo; shallowwaterflyfishing.com; John Stacy; Cortland Line Company; Henry Cowen; henrycowenflyfishing.com; Ross Reels; Temple Fork Outfitters; Captain Marcia Foosaner; Laura Pisano; Al Quattrocchi; tornadodesign.la; Alberto Knie, tacticalanglers.com; Paul Peluso; mamamiafishing.com; Don Avondolio; Captain Gordon Churchill; Justin Pellegrino; Jason Puris; Captain Vincent Catalano; joeyccharters.blogspot.com; Ken Ekelund; Tony Lyons; Jay Cassell; Bill Bowers; Kelsie Besaw; Pat Ford; patfordphotos.com; Bernard Lefty Kreh; Bob Clouser; Paul Schwack Jr.; Glenn Mikkleson; A.J. Forzano; Eric Peterson; Ray Bondorew; Lou Tabory; Stu Apte; Captain Al Ristori; Ray Stachelek. Thank you all.